MASTER FISHERMAN

PIKE

JOHN WATSON

MASTER FISHERMAN

PIKE

JOHN WATSON

WARD LOCK

Dedicated to Sally, my springer spaniel. No finer fishing companion could I ever have wished for.

© John Watson 1989

First published in Great Britain in 1989
by Ward Lock Limited, Artillery House, Artillery Row,
London SW1P 1RT, a Cassell Company

Edited by Richard Dawes
Designed by Ann Thompson
Illustrations by Peter Bull Art

Text filmset/set in 12 on 13½pt Times roman
by Fakenham Photosetting Limited, Fakenham, Norfolk.
Printed in Great Britain at The Bath Press, Avon

British Library Cataloguing in Publication Data
Watson, John
Pike. – (Master fisherman)
1. Pike. Angling
I. Title   II. Series
799.1′753

ISBN 0–7063–6791–X

CONTENTS

Mick Brown returns a 21½ lb (10 kg) livebait-caught pike to a Norfolk Broad.

CHAPTER ONE

THE PIKE ENTHUSIAST

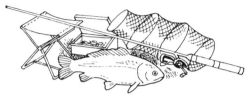

Man has always had a fear or hatred of the predator. The threat presented has often been due to the predator competing for the same food, although occasionally man himself has become that food! Naturally, man disliked the predator who killed his livestock, depriving him of the food he required to support his family. It is not surprising then that the pike still stirs up those ancient feelings of fear and hatred in the uninformed.

Fortunately, the majority of anglers have a more enlightened attitude towards the pike. In most situations the pike is no longer a competitor with man, but is itself now the subject of attention from the ultimate predator, man himself. Our particular form of predation, however, does not usually result in the death of the pike. Rather the pike enthusiast devotes all his efforts to the task of capturing the pike, and then releasing the fish soon after. The pleasure of the hunt is just the same whether the angler chooses to release or kill his quarry, but there are many anglers today who make it quite clear that letting the fish go unharmed gives additional pleasure. There is the motivation too that the fish might survive to be caught again by another angler, continue to grow, and perhaps reach specimen size.

A fighting fish

The pike, *Esox lucius*, is a worthy quarry, mainly because it is capable of putting up a very hard fight. Trout and salmon anglers can boast about the eating qualities of their quarry as well as the spectacular fight. We pike anglers are not interested in eating our catch, but can claim without fear of contradiction that pike can put up an arm-aching fight, sometimes so spectacular that some of the struggle occurs out of the water! The pike is also a pretty fish and though

7

beauty may well be in the eye of the beholder, all but the unfeeling could fail to admire the pike's perfect symmetry and the delicacy of its markings.

It would perhaps be going a little too far to describe the pike as an intelligent fish, for the species is governed by its instincts, with learned behaviour comprising only a very small part of its daily pattern of activity. Pike can learn to avoid baits in some waters, but this mainly occurs when their presentation is extremely unnatural. We anglers pit our wits against the factors which naturally work in the pike's favour. Pike are often quite timid and retiring and it is not difficult to scare them. They also eat only so much food in a year, some research suggesting that many days are spent with no need to go in search of food. Therefore we have to avoid scaring the pike and must also pick the times when it is hungry.

One of the biggest attractions of pike fishing is the variety of waters in which pike can be caught. Other anglers wax lyrical about the tranquil carp pool or the majestic sweep of a mighty salmon river. Pike anglers can enjoy all this and more because there are few waters where the species is not found. It is this wide choice of where we fish that makes pike fishing something special.

The mentality required to be successful with pike is difficult to describe. Perhaps the best comparison is with a top athlete or swimmer. The similarity between these high-profile professionals and the humble pike angler is clear: a huge amount of effort and self-denial is required to obtain the best results. To catch a few pike is not difficult, but to consistently catch big ones takes a lot of application. To continue catching big pike and to enjoy making the effort is even harder, and there are very few pike anglers in Britain who can claim to have done this. There is no need to go to extremes, but there is a certain breed of dedicated pike angler who is not content with accepting just what comes along.

Two decades of pike

My own pike fishing career extends back about twenty years, having started in my old home area of Blackpool in Lancashire. Such an area was never likely to turn me into a successful hunter of big pike, so I started to travel, tasting the delights of pike fishing in all of the countries of the British Isles and, along the way, most of the counties as well. Though pike fishing is not strictly specimen hunting, simply because you catch big pike by fishing for pike of all sizes, it is still possible to fish waters which have a reputation for big pike. This obviously increases your chance of catching a big fish, though other factors such as competition from like-minded anglers can make this more difficult.

My efforts over the years have yielded nearly seventy fish of over 20 lb (9 kg), which, compared with the efforts of other anglers around the country, is quite respectable. Of those pike, five were over 30 lb (14 kg), the best being the most recent: a fish of 38 lb 1 oz (17 kg). I feel lucky to have caught one thirty-pounder, so five makes me very happy indeed. Such fish are not widespread in England, though there are some waters where the chances are quite good, providing you can get a take!

Seasonal attractions

The time of year also has its influence on pike fishing. In much of England pike fishing is confined to the period 16 June–15 March. During these nine months you can enjoy lure fishing on quiet summer evenings or get up early on a June morning to go plug fishing on a Fen drain. Once autumn starts, with the air getting colder and mists starting to creep over the land, then classic pike fishing begins. Autumn leaves and frosts are very much a part of pike fishing and so are snow and ice in the margins of lakes and drains. Few fish species can be caught freely in such varied weather conditions. Furthermore, if you are able to travel to where there is no close season, then you can savour fishing on a fresh spring day, with nature once again coming to life.

The pike enthusiast can be a solitary character or can enjoy the pursuit of the fish as a part of a group of friends and fellow-anglers. Sometimes this social side of pike fishing brings out the worst in seemingly like-minded anglers. The desire to catch big pike can be such that corners are sometimes cut, which can obviously lead to bad feeling. My own attitude these days is to fish either with a good friend or on my own. It is possible, by keeping out of the way, to get the maximum enjoyment from the sport. This is after all why we go.

Of Britain's freshwater fish, the pike is most frequently the subject of legends and stories, the majority of which have been totally without factual foundation. Undoubtedly, the pike has been held in awe by many writers, angling and non-angling, over the years. Even modern-day poets such as Ted Hughes have been irresistibly drawn to writing about the fish. It is often the case that when we do not understand something, we fabricate a story so as to at least have a feeling of control over it. Then there are the mischief makers, those who would tell untruths and exaggerate simply because it is in their nature. The very fact that the pike has often been romanticized means that when delving into the history books we have to apply a fair degree of scepticism.

Getting at the facts

Even the subject of famous anglers and their catches of big pike leaves us with more questions than answers. This is simply because there have been many pike anglers who have, to be blunt, lied and lied again. To get a realistic picture of the facts relating to captures of big pike, it is best to consult an authority such as Fred Buller, who has spent many years collecting information relating to the pike and notable catches. Fred discovered, with the assistance of acknowledged fish scientists such as Alwyn Wheeler, that pike have existed in one form or another for at least sixty million years. Now when one considers that countless animal species have come and gone during this period, it is clear that the pike is a survivor.

The story of man's long association with the pike is not altogether clear, although ancient hunters were engraving pike onto their weapons about 17,000 years ago and they may well have hunted pike for at least 10,000 years before that. In those days sport was probably the last thing on their minds – the main object was to fill the stomach and avoid being eaten by anyone or anything else.

What then of the more recent pike angler? It is impossible to say for sure when rod-and-line fishing for pike started, but there are numerous references to it from the late 18th century, and by the start of the 20th century there were many pike anglers all over Britain. The national press certainly took note of some of the exploits of pike anglers, but it was not until the angling press evolved that detailed coverage of pike fishing began. Modern pike fishing evolved in the 1950s and appeared in its present form in the middle of the 1960s.

Since that period the main aspect of evolution has been the improved handling of the pike and the conservation of the species.

Recorded big pike

As far as the history of big pike captures is concerned, there has been so much fabrication and romance that it is now very difficult to distinguish fact from fiction. Fred Buller's list of big pike, for example, lists thirty-two fish over 50 lb (23 kg), yet not one picture is there to be seen of such a pike from the British Isles. It is true that there are impressive photographs of fish from, for example, Germany and Norway, so why none from Britain? Can we honestly believe that British anglers are too bashful to have their photograph taken? Or are many of the 50 lb (23 kg) pike recorded fakes or mistakes?

In areas such as southern Ireland there is scant regard for big pike and probably little grasp of the significance of a really big example.

A pike caught in the heyday of Hickling Broad — the early to middle 1960s.

But there is less of an excuse for the failure of British fish to feature in Fred Buller's list of big-pike captures. It is difficult for me and indeed unfair to dismiss his research, without doing my own studies along the same lines. So my opinion is purely a personal one and based on a basic understanding of human nature. When it comes to pike, as with other species, anglers are experts at exaggerating what they have caught. The evidence that pike can reach 50 lb (23 kg) or even 60 lb (27 kg) is not being disputed here. There have been enough good photographs of truly gigantic pike to convince even the sceptical that pike can grow to a very large size.

Sadly, in many ways conditions have changed in this country and many of the changes may have worked against the chances of any one water producing a really big pike. The most significant factor must have been the Industrial Revolution. Many of our rivers long ago ceased to be clean and this has several effects. First, many rivers have ceased to have a run of migratory fish species. Salmon and sea trout in particular are now very rare in major rivers such as the Trent and the Thames. Pollution has prevented these fish from running up rivers to spawn. Though salmon have been reintroduced to the Thames, there is a long way to go before conditions are favourable for large runs of such fish. On other rivers the netting of salmon at sea has reduced runs and even if the poor fish does manage to get to our estuaries it then has to contend with large-scale netting and poaching. The reduction in migratory fish is in effect a reduction of available food stocks for pike and could, in theory, result in the latter failing to attain a really large size. Certainly, this may offer some explanation of the fact that far fewer pike of over 40 lb (18 kg) are now reported in Scotland and Ireland.

Another significant factor is the increase in recent years in fishing pressure on pike. There are two types of such pressure. One is the simple increase in rod-and-line sport, the other is the pressure to exterminate pike on waters supposedly reserved for game fish. The fist type of pressure can be so intense on some waters that it leads to increased mortality in pike. While it is true that any fish species can tolerate the removal on purpose or by accident of a proportion of the stock, it is also true that pike rapidly succumb to mistreatment by careless anglers. To grow to a very large size a pike has to survive and, sadly, these days many very big fish are mishandled to such an

12

extent that their future hangs in the balance. In an ideal world, waters with giant-pike potential would be seldom visited by the pike angler. This, however, is far from being the case, for those waters with reputations for big pike rarely escape a tremendous onslaught and inevitably the fish are caught at least once.

The culling of pike

Other waters with big-pike potential are not given a chance. The majority of trout waters in England, Scotland, Wales and Ireland are managed with the aim of minimizing the number of pike present. The reason for this is that the management equate good trout fishing with minimal pike stocks. Regardless of whether this theory is valid or not, the net result is that most of these waters contain few pike and are generally not worth fishing. What most fishery managers fail to appreciate is the fact that both wild and natural trout populations have a natural mortality. Often, on English reservoirs, trout returns manage to reach around 80 per cent. This means that each year around 20 per cent of the trout stocked are not caught. What happens to these trout is unclear. If there are no pike present, then other types of predators, such as cormorants, may be responsible. Poaching or dishonest anglers may account for some, but whatever happens to the rest? Remember that on big trout waters we are dealing with 20 per cent of 50,000 fish, which is a lot of trout. If a trout fishery cannot obtain a higher return than 80 per cent without a pike population, then those trout waters getting this level of return with a pike population are going to waste a lot of time and effort removing pike.

It is even more ridiculous to try and exterminate pike in the giant Irish loughs. Yet since the mid 1960s large numbers of pike have been removed, supposedly to improve the trout fishing. Ironically, an interesting piece of research was carried out that showed that the demand for improved trout fishing was not there in the first place. With this perverse logic the Irish had ruined the best pike fishing in the world, which is now in demand, for a non-existent trout market. It would have been better if the Irish fisheries had made a bigger effort to advertise their trout fishing so as to draw revenue into the exchequer. However, far more seems to have been done to encourage the ordinary coarse angler.

Fortunately all is not lost, simply because Ireland's recent economic climate has ended pike removal. As a result the pike have started to recover in some of the western loughs and already British anglers are starting to catch some good fish there. In other parts of Ireland, however, visiting European anglers have done immense damage to pike stocks and some famous waters which did produce big pike are now a shadow of their former selves.

Although there is a lot of bad news, there are a few glimmers of light on the horizon. At the time of writing, I have just seen an exceptional two weeks' fishing on Llandegfedd reservoir in South Wales. Four pike of over 40 lb (18 kg) is enough to impress even the most hard-bitten pike angler. The main good news to come from this water was the Water Authority's decision that the big pike were to be returned. I think this reflects an appreciation of the sheer size of the pike present in the water. Any sensible angling administrator would think twice about destroying some of the biggest pike in the country just to placate some trout anglers. Trout there are plenty of; pike of over 40 lb (18 kg) are a different matter altogether.

Pike fishing in Europe

Even though Britain has proved itself capable of producing pike of this size, why do so many pike anglers still look to Europe for really big fish? It is an inescapable fact that waters in northern and central Europe have produced some huge pike in the 50–60 lb (23–27 kg) bracket. The waters around Amsterdam also produce some fish to 40 lb (18 kg), along with quite a few thirty-pounders (14 kg). However, when you analyse the results it is clear that the odds against a British angler going abroad and catching a fish of this magnitude are so great that it is not really worth considering. If even the most prolific country produced one pike of over 50 lb (23 kg) a year (which is by no means the case), there are thousands of pike anglers and many can fish every week. So the visitor fishing for, say, two weeks a year will be really lucky to get a fish even half that size.

Continental waters probably yield such huge pike because many fish do not survive very long. So many of these waters must contain only a few fish, thus producing the odd lucky pike which grows to colossal size. Another factor is that waters in, for example, Switzerland and Austria tend to be fairly cold and it seems that big pike

A 44½ lb (20 kg) pike caught by Carl Garratt at Llandegfedd in 1988.

prefer cooler waters to those that become very warm in the summer. Cool water also means a lower growth rate and a longer life. These large waters also contain many more prey fish species than those in Britain do, which again may help to produce fish of exceptional size. Not all the big foreign fish have been genuine. One character was claiming as rod-and-line captures pike which had been netted. As is so often the case, something leaked out and he was exposed.

A classic English counterpart is the case of the famous Whitehall pike. The story started with a reporter going to a taxidermist's studio to write a feature on the craft. There, he happened to stumble on a very large pike in the process of being mounted. The fish was almost finished, but yet to be placed in a case. The reporter questioned the taxidermist who simply replied that he could not reveal the details of the fish. For a while the matter rested. Then, unluckily for the *Angler's Mail*, someone decided that in the best traditions of investigative journalism the truth should be unearthed. Eventually the taxidermist, Roy Whitehall, decided to reveal that he had caught the fish from Lockwood Reservoir on the outskirts of London. Many local anglers would have accepted that this private water could produce a big pike, but when the weight of 43 lb 12 oz (20 kg) was announced there was consternation in the angling world. However, the story was published, along with a very dubious account of how the pike was caught.

A disputed record

The fish was then entered as a record contender since it was far heavier than the 40 lb (18 kg) pike caught by Peter Hancock in 1967. Even more unlikely was the fact that the British Record Fish Committee accepted this fish, which held the record for some time. However, some pike anglers in the know started to dig for information. Neville Fickling wrote to Alwyn Wheeler suggesting that the gill rays under the operculum appeared to be excessively stretched. The confirmation that the pike was a fake finally came when Martin Gay received a letter from an angler who had sent his 32 lb (14.5 kg) pike to Mr Whitehall to be set up. A comparison of the photographs of this fish and the 'record' confirmed that they were one and the same. The bogus record was thrown out; but a few years later the Whitehall pike was sold for a four-figure sum.

CHAPTER TWO

THE BIOLOGY OF THE PIKE

While many freshwater fish have failed to become totally adapted to their natural environment – a prime example is the salmon, which still has to return to the sea to feed after spawning – the pike can remain from birth to death in one water. Fish evolution has been such that long migrations have only become necessary because of competition from other species. Salmon spawn in freshwater streams because in the high reaches of a river there are few predators on the young fish and little competition for food and space. Pike on the other hand have evolved to survive in virtually any river or still-water, provided the river is not too fast and the still-water not too shallow. The pike's adaptability is the key to its widespread distribution. This adaptability is also reflected in the diverse nature of its diet and in its ability to reproduce successfully even in a relatively unfavourable environment.

SPAWNING

Life for the pike begins with the mating of male and female in the spring. In the British Isles spawning is usually carried out during late March or early April. There are exceptions, with some fish spawning as late as May. On rivers where the water is artificially warmed, such as the Trent, the pike appear in breeding condition earlier than in nearby still-waters, which suggests that the pike's biological clock is accelerated by warmer water. The factors governing spawning are certainly hormonal, for there are chemical messengers in the blood-stream which activate this and other behaviour. However, it is unclear whether day-length or temperature is the main factor. Pike certainly do show slight differences in spawning times depending on whether there has been a mild winter or not.

The author's rod lies on its makeshift rest in a peaceful spot on Loch Lomond's productive Ardlui Bay.

In my view, day-length is very significant, for otherwise pike would start spawning whenever the water temperature was right. Furthermore, it is not just the length of the day that is important, but also whether the daylight is increasing or decreasing in length. In March therefore the trigger will be an eleven-hour day, increasing in length as the month progresses, coupled with a rise in water temperature. Water temperatures are generally above 6 °C (43 °F) when pike spawn, and a figure of around 8 °C (46 °F) has often been quoted. The male and female pike seek suitable areas towards mid March. They need shallow water, heavily overgrown with reeds, grass and aquatic plants. It is on this sort of material that they spawn and from which they derive some cover from predators.

When pike are spawning such shallow areas are frequently devoid of other fish, owing to the coldness of the water. Even eels, which tend to be avid eaters of fish spawn, are dormant at this time of year. This situation improves the chances of survival of the pike eggs and

This 24 lb 10 oz (11 kg) gravid female was caught on a chub deadbait from a 2 ft-deep (0.6 m) swim on a Norfolk Broad.

fry, yet presents the adult pike with no problem because few of the adults are likely to want to feed during this period anyway.

Generally, each female will be larger than the males that accompany her. This may well be the reason why male pike seldom grow to over 12 lb (5.5 kg). It is thought that the act of fertilization of the eggs by the male requires eye-to-eye contact between male and female. If the male is shorter than the female then the sperm can be wafted over the eggs by the fin motions of the two fish. The eye contact between the larger females and shorter male ensures this.

The sight of pike spawning is quite remarkable. A female will sometimes have three or four consorts and they will all seem to be swimming as one fish. During a short period they will range far and wide over an area of suitable weed. Eggs are deposited here and there and never all at once in one area. If suitable spawning habitat is not available or if water temperatures fall below 5 °C (41 °F), then spawning can be delayed. Whether the pike move into deeper water

19

or simply stay put, is unclear, but once the temperature starts to rise, spawning recommences. The males suffer badly during this period, fighting among themselves. Also, the larger females often grab hold of the hapless suitor. Consequently many males are very badly marked. Fins become badly frayed and frequently extensive teeth marks can be seen near the tail. This sort of damage is inflicted on fish as large as 9 lb (4 kg).

Once the spawning is over, usually before the water temperature reaches 13 °C (55 °F), the pike move back out into deeper water until they return to feed on the perch when these move in to spawn. The eggs are laid on weed and are adhesive, which ensures that they do not fall to the bottom where silt would suffocate them. The length of time for hatching depends largely on the water temperature. Spawning sites are generally sheltered from the wind, but freak weather conditions can disturb weed growth or smother weed and eggs with silt. At 8 °C (46 °F) the eggs take seventeen days to hatch. If the temperature drops below 4 °C (39 °F) or exceeds 16 C (61 °F), high mortality results. Similarly, if water levels drop before the eggs hatch, they may all die as a result of drying.

An uncertain start

From the above it can be seen that nothing is guaranteed for the eggs of the pike and in some years almost all the eggs or young pike fail to survive. In some waters this situation may lead to very low stocks of pike, although it can result in rapid growth because of the lack of competition for food. Reservoirs in particular are prone to low water levels in the spring, while upland waters with few shallow areas may also present an environment inhospitable to pike.

EARLY DEVELOPMENT

Within a few hours of hatching, the pike fry are very active, but they soon attach themselves to the vegetation by means of an adhesive pad. They hang in this position while the yolk sac is absorbed. In spring, the invertebrate fauna is also on the increase and it is these very small organisms that provide the young pike with its first food. At first, rotifers, and then items such as *Daphnia*, are consumed by the fry. The tiny pike, only an inch (25 mm) long, then migrate away

A tiny but perfectly detailed pike.

from the spawning area to slightly deeper, but still weedy water. As spring becomes summer other fish species will have spawned in the shallow water.

The small pike, now 3 in (75 mm) long, is capable of eating other fish. It is a perfectly formed copy of the adult, complete with teeth and delicate bar markings. Some of the small pike grow more quickly than others, and if there are many young, then the slower-growing individuals become prey for their larger brothers and sisters. Cannibalism is one of nature's ways of adjusting the population to a size that the environment will support.

The individuals that eat their own kind frequently grow even faster, because of the sound economics of eating a solid meal. Although these small pike are already predators, they are not immune from the attention of other creatures. Dragonfly and beetle larvae have particularly nasty eating habits, sucking the hapless

21

young pike's body fluids until a mangled husk remains. Herons and grebes also take their toll, while the odd older pike may itself be hunting the shallows. Perch are fond of a diet of pike and no doubt at night the young pike do not rest easily as eels slither around looking for an easy meal.

Throughout the summer, growth continues and soon fish comprise almost all of the diet of the small pike. At times when fish prey are not available, water shrimps and the like may be eaten in large numbers. However such a diet does not allow rapid growth and underdeveloped pike may well invite the attentions of other, more fortunate, pike.

Winter growth is very limited and the young pike, now perhaps a foot (30 cm) long, try to remain near cover of weed. Forays out into open water inevitably result in exposure to larger pike. Where cover is very limited, the young pike frequently fail to show a good survival rate, because of the predations of the adults.

The pike's growth rate

The growth rate of pike is said to depend on a number of factors. Water temperature has been discussed as one key determinant. In the colder waters at the north of the pike's distribution range, growth can be very slow. The farther south, the faster, in general, is the growth rate. Other factors are food availability and the density of pike. So it is quite possible to have fairly fast-growing pike in northern latitudes and slow-growing pike farther south.

The longevity of pike is also related to water temperature. The farther north, and the slower the growth, the longer pike live. In Canada, where pike can grow very slowly for a long time, they can reach twenty-four years of age. In the south of the United States the majority are only four years old. This rule applies to some extent in Britain, Loch Lomond pike of up to eighteen years having been recorded. These old fish may weigh 30 lb (14 kg) and measure 4 ft (120 cm) in length. Farther south, in England, some trout-water pike may be six years younger, slightly shorter, and yet weigh substantially more. It is unclear whether or not these fish are short-lived, simply because people tend to kill or remove many pike from trout waters. Perhaps in the future we will have a chance to judge how these pike compare with their northern counterparts.

Feeding habits

Quite a lot of research has been done on the feeding of pike and during my time as secretary of the Pike Anglers' Club a number of interesting scientific papers passed through my hands. A lot of the work was contradictory, but the important point which came up again and again was that a pike will, when possible, take a prey item that gives it the biggest energy yield for the least effort. Energy is generally considered to be the number of calories produced from a unit of food. While it is true that different fish have different calorific values, it is not possible to claim with any certainty that particular prey species are more beneficial to the pike than others.

What is clear is that consumption of a fish of, say, 10–20 per cent of the pike's bodyweight is a highly efficient way of feeding. Compare this with the capture of, say, twenty fish each of 1 per cent of the weight of the pike, and it becomes clear that it is far more economical to feed on the larger food items. This makes sense in theory, but in reality such large prey items are not easily available in most waters. They are also more difficult to catch and keep hold of. If the pike had the choice it would always go for the larger prey fish, but more often than not it has to eat what it can find most easily. In complete contrast, pike sometimes feed very effectively on fry which, when densely packed, can be extremely easy to catch.

If we compare all the waters that have produced big pike in the past we see the same pattern again and again. The first, most significant, factor is that prey species are numerous and generally plentiful around the 1–2 lb (0.5–1 kg) mark. While there may be many smaller and some larger prey fish, most will be in this ideal size range. The species of prey fish does not matter very much, for big pike have turned up in waters holding bream, tench, roach, chub or trout. Trout waters are perhaps a special case, simply because fresh stocks are added every year. From the pike's point of view, this is ideal as most of the trout are around 1 lb (0.5 kg). In Ireland's western trout loughs there are plenty of 1–2 lb (0.5–1 kg) trout and their presence has a beneficial effect on the growth of the pike there. With the addition of migratory fish such as salmon it is not surprising that these waters have produced many pike over 40 lb (18 kg).

If the prey fish are mostly available during the pike's peak feeding period, April–June, then fast growth is almost a certainty. Imagine the situation: vast numbers of rainbow trout pushed into a water in the spring or big shoals of 2 lb (1 kg) bream spawning in June. Such easy feeding provides the sort of situation that will produce big fish. If there are very few pike feeding on a large good resource then it may well be even easier for the pike to capture food and this in turn may make rapid growth even more likely. Most of the very big pike of over 40 lb (18 kg) caught in Britain have been taken from waters heavily stocked with suitable prey, yet with small pike populations. This certainly applies to all the Thurne pike over this weight and the record pike of 44 lb 14 oz (20 kg) from Ardleigh, a water which has very good coarse-fish stocks and few pike because of netting and killing. The Llandegfedd pike over 40 lb (18 kg), of which there were two in the first season's fishing, were the top of a 'pyramid' of pike which is thought to have contained only a small number of fish.

If we are to see any further catches of big pike from new waters then the situation there will probably have to be as described above. As we have seen, in Europe the pike grow even bigger. However, in these waters are often found large shoals of fish we rarely come across in Britain. Whitefish, which are like our native powan, may average around 2 lb (1 kg) each and be very numerous, while most of the other food fish will also be of acceptable size. Many waters in Britain can produce 30 lb (14 kg) pike, but the circumstances would have to be very exceptional to produce fish of over 50 lb (23 kg). Those who talk glibly of such fish are living in a dream world.

Jim Gibbinson once made a very accurate observation about another factor that influences pike growth when he said that big pike thrive on neglect. A good pike water tucked away and undiscovered can throw up a very big fish. Yet it seldom does so after anglers start to hammer the water week in week out.

The hunt for food

Generally, any fish species has to move to some extent to find food. Herbivorous fish will graze an area and then move on to another. Predators can operate in a similar manner, but their prey can also move and this presents problems. The first thing a pike needs to do is to regularly find its prey fish. Instinct tells the pike where prey fish will be during each season. Loch Lomond pike, for example, no doubt 'know' that powan spawn on gravel areas in January and so make great use of this easy prey at that time. Similarly, pike follow spawning perch and roach into the shallows. Sometimes, this involves movements of several miles. (Pike have also been known to travel at least 5 miles (8 km) to find suitable spawning areas.)

Laboratory studies of the pike have shown that it does spend a lot of its time inactive. In some waters it is not difficult to confirm this by observation. Pike have three basic states: resting and not interested, resting and ready to feed, and hunting. The first is typical of pike once they have fed well and no longer wish to eat. This is the fish you find and cast a bait to with no result. Eventually, if you persist, the pike usually swims off in disgust, perhaps to find a nice quiet spot!

A more favourable proposition is the pike that has positioned itself so as to ambush prey. Pike frequently rest in reeds or on the bottom in areas where prey fish are likely to pass by. If you present a bait to a pike in the resting-but-willing-to-feed state then you more or less have it! Just lying around is without doubt energy-efficient, but it does not increase the pike's chance of a meal. It is therefore obvious that the pike has to go out and look for food from time to time. This it can do by slowly patrolling an area or by rapid swimming until it locates prey. In large, fairly barren waters this swimming phase is probably prolonged and perhaps accounts for the lean shape of the pike and its phenomenal fighting ability.

THE PIKE AND ITS PREY

The pike relies on one or more of three senses to locate its prey: sight, smell and hearing. That pike have good eyesight is without doubt, otherwise the eyes would not be as large. The pike has a reasonable range of vision around it, but the most useful area is probably just ahead of its snout. It is at the business end that the pike's vision is most important. Although sight is important, pike can also feed effectively in the dark and in very turbid water.

Smell may well be important in some situations, many pike anglers being convinced that this is the case. For nostrils, the pike has only a couple of blind holes on the snout, but angling experience shows that different types of deadbait can be distinguished remarkably well on some waters. The fact that many deadbaits look very similar suggests that it is scent that the pike is relying on.

Steve Redman took this lean fish from Portnellan Bay on Loch Lomond. A boat is useful on large waters such as this.

However, articles in American magazines on the subject, based on laboratory work, do not place a great emphasis on smell. Despite these findings, in situations where sight and sound cannot help a pike find prey, it must be smell that guides it to the dead or wounded fish lying on the bottom. Many fish species have been shown to be extremely sensitive to smells and without doubt a fish with only a moderately developed sense of smell would be well endowed if it came into our world.

Hearing or rather the ability to pick up vibrations underwater is probably highly important in pike. After all, the pike has an extension of the lateral line system, a series of pores on the head and along the underside of the jaw. Its hearing probably functions like its sense of smell in being a long-range 'radar that enables it to home in on prey before fixing them with its eyes for the final kill. Part of the effectiveness of lures is due to the sounds that they generate. Even from some distance – say, 20 ft (6 m) – a pike will hear a disturbance caused by prey or a lure. It takes very little time for the pike to sprint the short distance to the noise and investigate. It then has the option of attacking what it can now see with its eyes, or going back to waiting. My own experiments with throwing rocks into a water convinced me that pike can be very inquisitive and will often investigate unusual sounds.

The hearing of pike is also very evidently attuned to irregular vibrations such as those generated by a sickly fish or another pike feeding in the immediate vicinity. This is why when a used livebait is released a pike will frequently come in very quickly to grab it.

Built for speed

Going back to the movement of the pike, its body shape and muscles are designed mainly for very fast, short bursts of speed. No doubt a pike can chase fish for several minutes, but generally it is more energy-efficient to use its high speed from a standing start to capture a previously unaware fish. Many predators on both land and underwater have evolved this technique and proof of its effectiveness is provided by the millions of years that these sprinters have survived. In rivers pike do have to swim for long periods unless they can get well down near the bottom. There an area of slower-flowing water prevails and using this it is possible to 'stick' quite effectively to the river bed. However, once the pike is off the bottom, continuous swimming is essential otherwise it will be washed downriver.

Several factors can make pike move long distances and nowhere is this more evident than on the Norfolk Broads. Here prey fish tend to show seasonal movements and the pike must follow if a living is to be made. On the Thurne, for example, it has been noted that pike will travel 4–5 miles (6.5–8 km) off the broads and down the main river to the village of Potter Heigham. Similar movements in the reverse direction occur and part of the difficulty of pike fishing on this river is location of the pike. This movement generally occurs because the prey fish make a similar move.

On the Bure similar movements can be noted in winter, and on both the Thurne and the Bure, the sudden appearance of a very big pike can generally be explained by a fish moving off an otherwise private broad for the first time that season. Without doubt, pike will often stay put in an ideal environment with plenty of food and lack of disturbance from boats and anglers. However, very cold weather sometimes makes them move to more favourable areas.

The shock of being caught can also contribute to the movement of pike. How often does a really productive area go dead after intense fishing pressure? The pike could be off the feed, but more often than not the same fish turn up somewhere else, quite clearly having moved, sometimes as much as 6–7 miles (9.5–11 km). Movement over considerable distances is something we must expect from all fish, because although it has been demonstrated again and again that many fish have a restricted area of movement (their 'home range') some must move long distances, otherwise colonization of new or unpolluted waters would never occur.

How pike arrive in still-waters is still something of a mystery. Obviously a little human help is not unusual, because man has been moving fish around for centuries. However, there are still-waters, remote and well away from others holding pike, which seem unlikely to have been stocked by man. The theory that water birds carry weed with spawn attached might well be valid, but no one can really confirm or refute it. During floods, when rivers run into otherwise unconnected lakes, pike obviously move back and forth, and this solves part of the mystery. Sometimes, in large reservoirs, pike appear very quickly after flooding, but pumping operations to fill these storage reservoirs are frequently the explanation. Eggs or pike fry are easily moved via pumps and pipelines, in what is a passive rather than an active movement. When adult pike arrive suddenly in a top trout water, the only explanation can be the work of anglers. No one, in my view, can condone this sort of action, but on the other hand it is hard to be happy about trout-fishery managers who kill big pike and sell them to the fishmongers.

Self-selected coloration

An interesting topic for the angler interested in just a little more than catching pike is the fish's coloration. Many fish species show colour variations from water to water and brown trout, for example, are known for their variability. Pike are also extremely diversely coloured and the reasons for this lie initially with the environment. Though there are exceptions to the rule, pike in each water tend to have very characteristic colours and marking, which can be totally different from those in even nearby waters. It is well known that a fish can determine its own pigmentation balance and thus its colour. It seems to be the case that every pike's eye can judge what is the optimum coloration for its own needs. There are two aspects to this variation in colour: long-term coloration and short-term. Most fish can alter the second at any time of the day. Presumably this is to suit variations in light intensity under water. For example, on days when a pike may need to appear lighter in colour, its skin can make this change as required. The change back to darker colours is equally easy. You only have to put livebaits in a white bucket and then release them into the lake to see that they have adjusted their coloration accordingly.

Long-term colour changes are something that I do not fully under-stand. There are several questions that remain unanswered. For example, is the eventual colour and spot-pattern of the pike genetic and passed on from its parents? Or does the environment shape the coloration and marking of the pike? Without doing some experiments, all I can do is guess that it might be a little bit of both.

The variation in marking and colour is most obvious if you have fished around a bit. River Bure pike are generally brown, with very yellow, nearly orange, spots. The spots tend to be vivid, showing up well and making the fish very attractive. Thurne pike can also be

29

vividly marked, but are often green with less obvious spots. In Ireland spots become stripes, while I understand from anglers who have fished in Holland that some pike are virtually striped all along their body, with few spots evident. Loch Lomond pike are green, with generally numerous small spots, while pike from some of the Midland reservoirs have vivid markings which become swirling spots and stripes around the tail. When the pike starts life the spots are basic vertical bars, but as time goes by these break up into spots.

With large pike which have ceased to grow rapidly it is possible to use the spots to identify individual fish. This method has long been used to provide interesting information on pike stocks in various waters. I am not bothered myself about identifying individual fish because I seldom fish any water long enough to enable me to build up a long-term picture of the growth of particular pike.

Unnatural development

Some pike show unusual physical characteristics and most pike anglers will have come across a variety of 'freaks' over the years. Generally, such pike are lucky to have survived because nature tends to weed out the imperfect very quickly. Those which do survive are obviously not seriously affected by their deformity, although these fish may be very slow-growing and fail to reach a large size. An oddity which turns up from time to time is the pug-nosed pike. These fish have a convex, rather than concave, upper jaw. This is often much shorter than the lower jaw so that the latter protrudes a long way. Such fish are very odd-looking and I believe they are common in Ireland, but less so in Britain.

Another jaw deformity is found in the pike with both jaws up-turned. This gives the unfortunate animal an almost comic look and it could certainly be imagined that the fish had a big smile on its face. The degree of upturning is variable, but I have seen some extreme examples in other anglers' photographs. Two-tone pike are not uncommon, with one side of the pike being lighter than the other. A malfunction in the pike's brain probably caused the short-term coloration to be incorrect on one side of the fish. Blind pike are invariably pitch-black and it is common to find pike which are blind in one eye. These fish will sometimes be a strange colour, totally different from the other fish in the water.

The author displays a sleek fish of about 13 lb (6 kg) caught on a shallow-fished livebait at the height of the summer.

Deformed backbones lead to all sorts of oddities. There are some pike the shape of a banana; that is, they have a bend in the body which results in the head and tail being much lower than the middle of the back. Others simply have a big bump behind the head. 'Quasimodo', a pike I saw caught at Swithland Reservoir, had a huge growth behind its head, which eventually burst and caused its death. Some pike have a shortened backbone, so that the tail appears to be stuck on to the body two-thirds of the way along it. Some of these fish are very fat and look almost like carp. Many pike suffer from small bumps and growths. Often very old fish have them and they can sometimes lead to the death of the fish. The freaks of nature are all very interesting, but the biggest question most pike anglers will want an answer to, is, why does a certain water produce a really big pike, while another does not? Also, what determines the number of pike in a water? A little speculation might provide one or two answers. There are waters which produce 20 lb-plus (9 kg) pike, but seldom, if ever, yield a big one; say, a thirty-pounder (14 kg). Some waters are excellent for fish over 10 lb (4.5 kg), yet have little chance of producing a twenty-pounder (9 kg).

The reason for this will almost certainly be the fact that there are too many pike in the water. They are chasing a limited number of food fish around and it is simply not possible for any individual fish to get sufficient easy food of the right size to grow really large. By contrast, there are some waters, such as the Thurne, which have a very low pike population and this may give rise to much bigger fish, simply because food is easy to obtain. Also, where the spawning habitat limits the numbers of young pike which arrive each year, it is unlikely that these would show the reduction in growth associated with large numbers of young.

One thing is certain: many waters change over the years and it is quite possible for a water to have a brief period when it produces some huge pike. This period may not be repeated for many years, so if you do stumble on such a water it can pay to fish it as much as possible. The chance of a big fish may not come around again.

The largest of these Bure winter pike, 23½ lb (10.5 kg), fell to a paternostered live dace; the others, 15½ lb and 15¾ lb (7 kg), to a trolled livebait.

Above Dave Plummer with a Loch Lomond pike taken on paternostered livebait.
Top right A collection of home-made sliding floats.
Right Measuring the author's best pike, 38 lb 1 oz (17 kg).

David Pond of Norwich proudly displays a superb Bure pike of 26½ lb (12 kg) which he took on a half mackerel.

CHAPTER THREE

THE PIKE'S HABITAT

It would be much easier if we could regularly go underwater, searching out the pike we seek to catch. We could easily learn what it is that attracts pike and why so often large numbers inhabit one small area. Unfortunately, this is not generally possible, although some anglers are keen divers, for in most waters in Britain visibility is such that sub-surface investigation would not prove to be very illuminating. Moreover, in some ways it would detract from the fun of fishing if we knew too much, because part of the game is to make deductions based on exploration and sometimes guesswork, with a little luck thrown in for good measure.

Population structure

In a normal pike water the population can be seen as a pyramid. To give a simple example, we could guess that in one water there would be fifty fish up to 3 lb (1.35 kg), twenty-five fish up to 6 lb (2.7 kg) and a mere ten fish below 10 lb (4.5 kg). Then there might be five or six of 10–19 lb (4.5–8.5 kg) and one twenty-pounder (9 kg). These pike will not be spread around in the water like currants in a bun. They will be distributed in a way typical of pike. The small fish, say up to 3 lb (1.35 kg), will be hidden in the weed or sheltering in reedbeds, while the larger fish will be lumped together in a few well-defined areas. They will be concentrated in certain areas simply because these offer something that others do not.

Although pike have to spend some time hunting for food, in each water there will be certain areas which present the best starting-point for a hunt and these will often be usefully located for the odd passing meal! Areas favoured by the larger pike may also provide a certain type of cover.

Pike love areas of non-conformity in waters which are otherwise

The crowning glory of the author's pike career: a fish of 38 lb 1 oz (17 kg) caught on a whole herring from Norfolk's Thurne system.

uniform. In winter, it is all very well fishing in weedbeds and the reeds, but the big pike may be way out in the lake or holed up or tucked in against a steep-sided gravel bar. The angler who fishes the weedy water may catch pike, but frequently the best he will manage to catch are the very small fish sheltering from the big pike.

BROADLAND PIKE

On a typical Norfolk Broad, barren of weed and heavily silted, it is not always easy to imagine where the pike are. However, if you take the trouble to plumb the depths and explore the margins where trees overhang, it is possible to find some features which may well hold pike. My first thirty-pounder (14 kg) came from a fairly shallow broad, but the swim, discovered by accident, was just a bit deeper than the water elsewhere. On broads lacking any obvious features the importance of moving around cannot be overstressed. Here a boat allows you to fish all areas without having to carry tackle a long way and to fish a lot of water in a day.

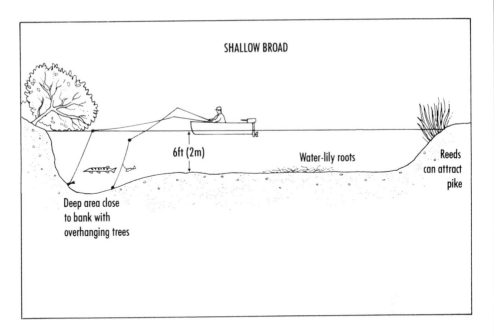

SHALLOW BROAD

6ft (2m)

Water-lily roots

Reeds
can attract
pike

Deep area close
to bank with
overhanging trees

Some broads are very weedy, and faced with beds of identical weed it is hard to know where to start. But one thing is certain: if there are many pike in the water and the water is shallow and weedy, they will be in the weed. Pike, being sensible fish, do not like to expose themselves in daylight and tend to stay in the weed unless hunting, and even then they frequently hunt from bed to bed. In deeper waters the depth itself provides cover, but on shallow waters weed can be very important. Do not be afraid to cast into or near weed, for the simple reason that a food item dropped on a pike's head will seldom be refused. However, in such situations there are problems with bait presentation and getting the pike out.

In the case of shallow, weedy broads (see diagram above), it is difficult to say where the pike will turn up. When they are on the hunt they can appear just about anywhere, often swirling and, in so doing, betraying themselves. When they are less active and at rest it is only possible to spot a pike if you happen to get too close and one actually swirls as the boat approaches. Areas worthy of attention are the great floating mats of Norfolk reed. Big pike can end up resting under these, and several times I have hooked big fish which seemed to be interested only in getting to the shelter of these areas.

At other times a bait presented in a slightly deeper, but almost weed-free area, is taken with gusto by surprisingly big fish. These clear areas are worth trying at the very start or end of the day, because poor light is another form of cover that pike are very willing to take advantage of.

Never stay all day in one spot if you are not getting any action. Many times I have moved from an unproductive area and been rewarded with some very big fish in another spot. Needless to say, there are exceptions to this rule and there have been times when, fishing a known big-pike swim, I have had to sit it out and wait for the pike to feed. Such spots are well known on waters such as Martham Broad, where you have to fish at one of a small number of allocated swims. Here it may take all day to get one run, but if it is a twenty-pounder (9 kg), then I for one will not complain! This situation is rather frustrating, though, because most anglers who fish this water know that they would have a far better chance by moving around and trying other 'illegal' swims.

Roving tactics

On very large broads such as Hickling, Horsey and Heigham, you must assume that the pike will feed if you find them. On these waters pike are so few and far between that the sit-and-wait approach does not pay off. You have to cover as much water as possible, in order to have any chance of putting a bait to a pike. Where pike are seldom caught, it is hard to build up a picture of where their favourite haunts are. It is useful to have records of where fish were caught in the past, but the best tactic is to try everywhere at least once. You may find pike out in open water or up against the reeds or in the depths of beds of mare's tail.

The time of year also has a big bearing on the location of pike on the broads themselves. There is definite evidence that during the summer big pike will be found there in numbers. However, where connection to the river system is well defined, cold weather or angling pressure can move them off. When time is limited, it is sometimes difficult to know which is better: broad or river. A nice short-cut that I have used occasionally is to set a few deadbaits on lengths of cotton, with small pieces of polystyrene as floating markers. With these scattered around the likely fishing areas it is possible to see if any pike have been about. This tactic led to the capture of my best pike, a fish of 38 lb 1 oz (17 kg). Eels can make this tactic unworkable as they will happily take the baits, giving the impression that the water is well endowed with pike.

An alternative approach is to pay attention to the signs that betray the presence of prey fish. Often, you may be driving back from a day's fishing at dusk and notice a concentration of fish on the surface. This is typical of roach, and if the shoal stays put for a long time, there is every chance that some pike will have moved into the area. If a broad appears totally dead and no food fish are seen and no pike are caught, it may well be that they have all moved off. It is the angler who can make the right decision at this point who continues to catch fish.

If both prey fish and pike move off, they generally head for an area with a feature. Features on broadland rivers are not uncommon. These can be boat dykes or areas of river sheltered from the worst of the cold winds by buildings or trees. The first people to spot these migrations are usually the match anglers. So it is always worthwhile scanning the local and national angling reports to see what has been going on. If the 'maggot anglers' are catching well for several weeks, then get down there.

Food-fish concentrations

Some of the concentrations of roach and bream are enormous. On the Thurne at Potter Heigham, in Herbert Wood's boatyard, thousands of fish pack in during each winter. Such places (see diagram on page 38) provide brilliant coarse fishing and sometimes the pike are not far away. I say sometimes, simply because angling pressure soon disperses the limited number of pike and it can be a long job trying to catch fish that are now miles away.

No one knows how pike manage to arrive where the food fish are, but they do have an uncanny knack of doing it time and time again. The daily movements of pike probably bring them into contact with big shoals of fish and once contact is established it can be maintained. However, the longer-distance movements may be imprinted in the pike's memory, a characteristic behaviour for the fish in that water. Just once in a while you come across broads which are not uniform. This situation arises where silt has been removed. For

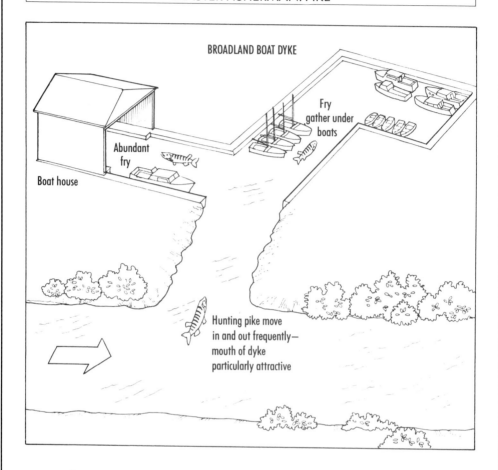

BROADLAND BOAT DYKE

Fry gather under boats

Abundant fry

Boat house

Hunting pike move in and out frequently— mouth of dyke particularly attractive

example, on Rockland Broad there is a distinct deeper channel. Now, before the reader thinks that is another deep channel that will later prove to be a figment of the writer's imagination, I must say that I am writing this book from experience, not hearsay. The channel on Rockland does exist and the plumbing I did there proved it. Because the water is tidal and can be very shallow at times, the pike can concentrate in the deeper channel. When the tide was up, the shallow areas were deep enough to allow freedom of movement. A similar situation may well have prevailed on Martham Broad, because that too is tidal.

On the Ormesby Broad system, which is landlocked and not connected to any major waterway, the depth of the water tends to vary considerably from broad to broad. Generally, there is a lot of uniform, often shallow, water. But by using the echo-sounder it is possible to find interesting areas where the bottom is gravel rather than mud, areas where there is a sudden depth change, or deeper water close to reeds. It takes very little effort to locate such features, but they make fishing so much more productive, compared with fishing 'blind'.

LOCATING PIKE IN RIVERS AND DRAINS

Rivers present a variety of problems. Let us first look at the fast-flowing type of river (see diagram on page 41). There are many of these around the country and most hold big pike. There is a common assumption that big pike in rivers like slack water. While big pike may be caught from slack water, it is generally true that it is easier to fish such areas of a river and this is why more pike are caught there than elsewhere. Big pike can hold station quite effectively in fast water, although turbulent water is a different proposition. To hold station the pike will generally stick on the bottom, but too much swirling of water makes this difficult. Yet on the Severn pike can be caught right under the sills of weirpools. The water in such spots is in fact probably relatively calm, giving the pike a suitable position from which to strike out into the more turbulent areas of the river. If you are equipped to fish fast water, then you will catch them there as well.

In Broadland only the Wensum is a truly fast-flowing river, although the tidal Waveney is good competition for it. On either water you need to fish in such a way that, if required, the bait stays put. To do this you need a combination of plenty of weight and as little line resistance as possible. The areas I always look at first on the rivers I have fished are those with strong features.

A little later you might well fish less obvious swims and still catch some good fish. However, big bends with undercut banks, deep holes and spots with overhanging or fallen trees are all worth looking at. Overhanging trees in particular can harbour shoals of fry. In the really fast-flowing rivers cover for pike can be at a bare minimum: for example, a large boulder in the middle. A pike will use such cover and, in addition, the shelter from the current enables it to lie off the bottom without much expenditure of energy.

A 16 lb (7 kg) fish taken in good condition from a Norfolk river by the author.

Many fast-flowing rivers have over the years been dredged and disturbed in other ways. Consequently, some do not present the angler with much scope for locating pike. Over-widened rivers tend to silt up quickly and can soon become shallow and virtually lifeless. Features which provide cover, such as trees, reeds and weeds, are frequently ripped out. Even weirs are being removed from some rivers and this gives the fish very little chance to find a section suitable to live in. Tidal rivers, because they are deeper and generally much wider than non-tidal rivers, are more uniform anyway and lack obvious features.

Underwater, all the usual rules apply, with deep holes and sometimes sunken trees being fish-holding features. Rivers such as the Waveney are not easy to fish because of the lack of these features. There is also the problem of knowing whether or not your presentation is effective. In fast, heavily coloured water your bait could be all but invisible. Fortunately you can rely on the pike's sense of smell to solve that problem. This is one reason why oily sea-fish baits have proved so effective on this river.

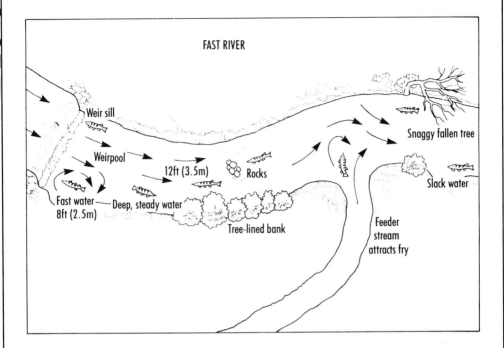

FAST RIVER

Weir sill

Weirpool

12ft (3.5m)

Rocks

Fast water — Deep, steady water
8ft (2.5m)

Tree-lined bank

Snaggy fallen tree

Slack water

Feeder
stream
attracts fry

Pike are fairly tolerant of saline conditions and can live in brackish water. This has a big bearing on fishing tidal rivers, simply because high tides can turn freshwater into sea water. This sort of salt influx is too drastic for any freshwater fish to be able to adapt to and generally pike move smartly upstream. They either do this or die. A simple test on arriving at the river is to taste a drop of water on your finger. If you can taste salt then be warned: you might do better going after cod! However, because pike are tolerant of brackish water, do not dismiss the possibility that there might be fish further downriver than is generally thought likely. Unfortunately time is often too limited to explore for pike at the margins of their range, so such areas are generally overlooked.

Fishing drains

Fen drains may be very different from fast-flowing rivers, but a lot of pike anglers carry out their pursuit on such waters (see diagram on page 42). Each drain fishes differently from the next. On the very small drains, such as those that feed the main drains, pike often exist quite happily in only 3 ft (1 m) of water. If the water has some colour or weed, they will make use of this cover. If there are plenty of reeds alongside the drain, even better. Many of the small drains are only 10 yards (9 m) wide, but they are sometimes several miles long. The problem is finding that comparatively short length of deeper water where the pike are. Deeper sections can only be found by fishing or plumbing the depth. Once these areas have been located it is common to find large numbers of pike. That extra depth, be it only a foot (30 cm), is all that is required to attract pike.

The larger drains, such as the Old Bedford and Vernatt's Drain, are featureless to the point of boredom, and when you are dealing with many miles of water, location becomes a daunting proposition. On waters like these, most anglers end up making use of information derived from other anglers. The good areas are often known; it is just a case of getting someone to part with that information! Sometimes a trip out in a boat can well solve the location problem. The

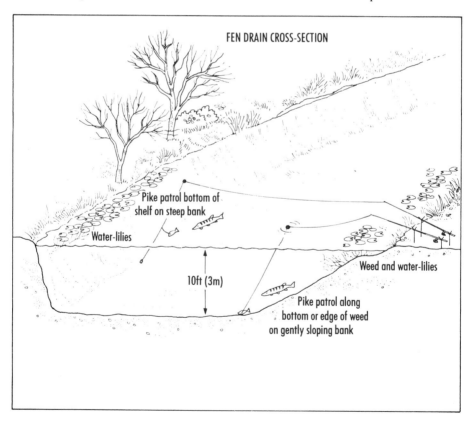

FEN DRAIN CROSS-SECTION

Pike patrol bottom of shelf on steep bank

Water-lilies

Weed and water-lilies

10ft (3m)

Pike patrol along bottom or edge of weed on gently sloping bank

Old Bedford today is very variable along its length. Some of it is weedy, some is so shallow the bottom can be seen, while the rest is a filthy brown. The best bet is to fish where the weed is and forget the rest. Where it is allowed, driving alongside a drain can provide plenty of information with the minimum of effort.

Some drains, such as the Delph, produce pike in many areas, although the big fish are not always widespread. An interesting aside concerning the Delph is the fact that it has from time to time been seriously polluted by summer flooding of the adjacent washland. When water stands on grass for any length of time in the summer it becomes deoxygenated, and when it runs back into the river a lot of fish can die, leaving the rest to flourish. This may be why the Delph has produced some pike exceptional for Fenland. In a few other Fen drains, natural or man-made disasters have contributed to such brief moments of glory and these occurrences are worth looking out for.

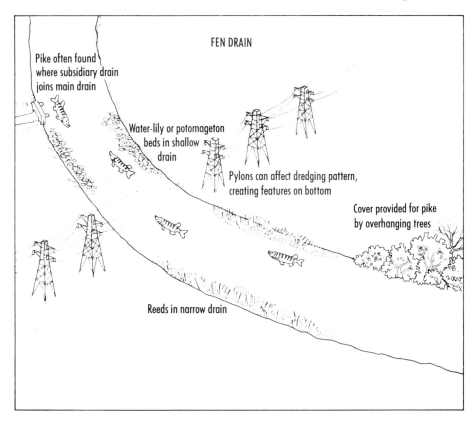

FEN DRAIN

Pike often found where subsidiary drain joins main drain

Water-lily or potomageton beds in shallow drain

Pylons can affect dredging pattern, creating features on bottom

Cover provided for pike by overhanging trees

Reeds in narrow drain

Pike location on waters such as the Delph, which is deeper than most Fen drains, is much more dependent on hard work than on water craft (see diagram on page 43). It does not take long to get to know the key areas where pike are most often caught, but such areas often have very little to differentiate them from others. Fortunately the Delph is an unusual water. Drains such as the Sixteen Foot and Middle Level are more obviously endowed with pike-holding areas: reedbeds, inflowing drains, or the junction of major drains can all mark good pike swims. In the late 1970s there were many areas of lily and weed cover, but, following dredging, such potential fish-holding features are now rare.

GRAVEL PITS AND RESERVOIRS

A much easier proposition than many waters, gravel pits have the advantage that once you have located the depths you can get to know the water fairly quickly (see diagram opposite). Pike like to patrol along bars and avoid swimming over them unless the water is very coloured. They also like flooded trees and bushes. Bays which attract fry are also key features. Generally, the clearer the water, the weedier it will be. Most water plants struggle to grow at depths below 12 ft (3.5 m) and some pits are almost barren at 25 ft (7.5 m). It pays therefore to start by exploring the areas which have features such as weed and gravel bars. Casting aimlessly out into a flat area with a depth of 25 ft (7.5 m) is not recommended.

Gravel pits with coloured water are a little different, because weed will generally be sparse and the only features left will be depth variations. Even then, some pits are solid with depth variations and there is no telling which feature will be attractive to pike without actually fishing first. If you have a boat, the technique of using deadbaits on cotton mentioned above can help here. On very clear pits the pike can be difficult to locate close-in, while in coloured water they can be caught right under your feet. Once again cover is the key to the pike's survival. Pike are some of the first fish to colonize a gravel pit and big pike can soon appear. The crucial factor is usually the appearance of perch, which multiply rapidly, providing a food base for the pike which soon follow.

Many gravel pits these days are used for a variety of non-fishing

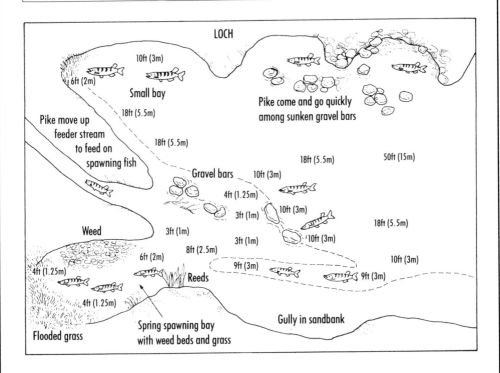

LOCH

10ft (3m)

6ft (2m)

Small bay

18ft (5.5m)

Pike come and go quickly
among sunken gravel bars

Pike move up
feeder stream
to feed on
spawning fish

18ft (5.5m)

Gravel bars   10ft (3m)

18ft (5.5m)   50ft (15m)

4ft (1.25m)

3ft (1m)   10ft (3m)

18ft (5.5m)

Weed   3ft (1m)

3ft (1m)   10ft (3m)

8ft (2.5m)

6ft (2m)

9ft (3m)   10ft (3m)

4ft (1.25m)

Reeds   9ft (3m)

4ft (1.25m)

Gully in sandbank

Flooded grass

Spring spawning bay
with weed beds and grass

pursuits. They are also used for cage farming of trout and this can have a very interesting effect. The trout are held in net cages and automatic feeders supply the food. This consists of pellets and each time the feeder is operated the odd pellet falls past the trout. Also, excretion by the trout results in the area around the cage being much more productive than elsewhere. Pike favour areas with cages because of the coarse fish they attract and, of course, the cover they can provide. Even when a cage is no longer in use, the structure itself can attract shoals of fodder fish. Cages are not restricted to just gravel pits, but are also used on the larger reservoirs. Here they are usually set in much deeper water, although the degree of attraction remains the same.

Pike in reservoirs

Reservoir pike have a vast expanse of water to move around in and so location can present greater problems. Most reservoirs follow a set pattern of shape and depth contours. The shallow water is at the inflowing stream end, while the deeper water is at the dam end.

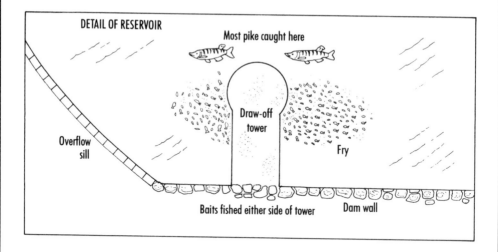

DETAIL OF RESERVOIR

Most pike caught here

Draw-off tower

Overflow sill

Fry

Baits fished either side of tower   Dam wall

Generally, the food fish are very widely spread around the reservoir in the summer and because of this the pike are also thinly scattered. The year's fry in particular will be scattered around the margins, using weed for cover. However, as the weed dies the small fish tend to congregate where there is a feature, in huge shoals that provide safety in numbers. Features that attract pike include draw-off towers and the deep water near the dam (see diagram above). Once these shoals have become established for a while, larger fish often gather in the same area. The pike are not slow to realize this and soon many will converge in the same area. Pike activity is often obvious, with strikes and swirls all over the place. It may seem to be totally uneconomical for pike to feed on fry shoals, but the tactics are to ingest as many fish as possible in one mouthful. This hit-and-miss method seems to work very well, so that fry-feeding pike can be very fat. However, it has the result that they can also be very difficult to tempt.

On some reservoirs this may not happen, some of the pike feeding instead on quite large prey fish, including tench and bream of around 2 lb (1 kg). The result is that these pike are often scattered around the water. Underwater features such as old roads, walls and hedges can be good points to ambush prey and many pike have been caught around such features. Reservoir pike can be found at a wide range of depths and they certainly seem able to exploit most of the water. Depths of down to 40 ft (12 m) have produced pike regularly

A nice bag of pike of mixed size, the biggest about 15 lb (7 kg).

on many waters, though most reservoir pike seem to come from around 20 ft (6 m). When the need arises pike will quite happily switch to feeding high in the water, especially when feeding on fry. Generally, however, they do not move into shallow water outside of the spawning period.

The finest of Britain's pike are probably those that live in the really big still-waters. These pike have a life pattern different from that of most other pike. Most of the really big waters hold comparatively few food fish. This means that pike hunt over much greater areas and once food has been found the attack must be quick and decisive. The infrequency with which food is encountered may not be too much of a problem, simply because food fish in these big waters tend to be of a reasonable size. If shoal fish such as roach and bream are not around, there is always the chance of a roaming trout, for these tend to swim vast distances searching for food and are therefore likely to be encountered regularly.

Ambush points

There is some evidence to suggest that these big-water pike tend to stop off at good ambush points and, once they have fed, move off again. Rocky points are areas where prey fish frequently pass and if there are boulders strewn around on the shelf a pike can rest almost unseen until an opportunity arises. Submarine bars and plateaux offer similar advantages. Where rivers run into a big water there is frequently a very extensive sandbank and migratory fish have to swim out onto the sandbank to gain entry to the river. Here again pike can lie in wait on the drop-off, particularly in October and November, when trout and salmon are running upriver. There are sometimes sunken trees washed down by floods in these areas and underwater films have shown quite clearly that pike use these very effectively as cover.

As mentioned earlier, pike move into shallow water during the spring, first to spawn and then to feed on other fish. Many Scottish and Irish waters can be fished during this period, and location is much easier at this time of the year. The shallow-water migration tends to concentrate the pike into a much smaller area, giving the pike angler his best chance of the year. These shallow areas are almost always the result of flooding from rivers and are frequently weedy and littered with snags.

Water quality

The biggest significant factor affecting pike in all waters is the quality of the water. Pike are fairly demanding when it comes to water quality and they do not generally fare well in polluted waters. There is some possibility that pesticides or heavy metals concentrate in pike because the fish are at the top of the food chain. Pike certainly need plenty of oxygen and a poor environment results in a smaller number of food fish. Nearly all the big pike that are caught each year come from waters with good-quality water. Therefore it is important that, as pike anglers, we support all those fighting to keep our waters clean. Without clean water we will be deprived of the enjoyment that a big pike provides.

The author returns his 38 lb 1 oz (17 kg) pike with the help of fellow pike enthusiast Bob Jackson.

This 24 lb (11 kg) fish from Vernatt's Drain, near Spalding, Lincolnshire, was at the time (February 1976) the author's best pike to date.

David Pond with a fine pike of about 14 lb (6.5 kg) which he took on a livebait during the summer of 1984.

An attractively marked 17 lb (7.5 kg) pike caught by the author on perch livebait from a shallow bay on Loch Lomond.

CHAPTER FOUR

TACKLE

Any angler who has fished for pike for over twenty years, as I have, should by now have strong ideas as to what constitutes good and effective pike-fishing tackle. It is obvious that some firms are selling tackle that leaves a lot to be desired, but I can only comment on what I have used and what I still use. It is then up to the reader to decide whether or not to take my advice.

RODS

These are probably the single most expensive item of tackle. Like most anglers I have graduated from glass-fibre rods to the latest carbon models. To be realistic, in the old days we caught pike very effectively on glass rods and today we do so on carbon rods. Some might ask, 'What's the point in paying £60 more for a carbon rod, when a glass one will do?' This is indeed a fair question, but one easily answered by anyone who has changed over from glass to carbon. Glass-fibre rods are much heavier because more material is required to give the rod sufficient stiffness to do the job in hand. Because top-quality carbon is much stiffer, it is possible to use less material, thus making the rod lighter and much nicer to use. Another benefit of carbon is the feel of the rod: everything seems much more positive and, particularly when you are lure fishing or wobbling deadbaits, the rod becomes an extension of your arm. All this serves to make for a more confident angler, who consequently puts more fish on the bank.

Rod length

The length of rods has also changed over the years. In the 1960s 10 ft (305 cm) rods were the order of the day, but this soon became 11 ft

(335 cm) and then 12 ft (365 cm). This last length assists long-distance casting and also gives a far greater degree of control when you are bank fishing reed-lined swims or fishing at close quarters from a boat. I would certainly be loath to go back to the shorter rods. My chosen rods these days are by Bruce and Walker and I have put my name to them. There are two versions: one is a 2¾ lb (1.2 kg) test-curve rod, ideal for all general purpose pike fishing; the other a 3½ lb (1.6 kg) rod for the bigger waters such as Loch Lomond, where bigger baits may be required, along with heavier lines and hard casting. Needless to say, these rods are fitted out with Fuji-type rings, which last forever without grooving. Most pike anglers use three rods, even though in some areas the Water Authority rules prohibit this. Most of these rules have been made by people who know little about our type of fishing and consequently most pike anglers disregard these silly restrictions. Three rods enables an angler to fish three different baits or presentations and this helps to sort out more quickly the feeding patterns of pike on a water.

Some people wonder why we have to use such powerful rods. Well, it is not because we need a stout rod to land the pike. Once in a while, perhaps, a fish will have to be dragged kicking out of a weedbed, but generally a powerful rod is needed to handle the baits and weight used to present them, whether they are live or dead. When you consider that the average livebait or deadbait weighs perhaps 3–4 oz (85–110 g) and the lead may weigh as much as 2 oz (60 g), then you can see that the pike angler is throwing the same weights around as the shore fisherman. The latter has a much more powerful rod, but then he has strong tides to contend with as well as weed, and sometimes very big fish.

REELS

Nowadays reels come in a hundred different shapes and sizes, yet when I started pike fishing there were only a handful of reliable models on the market. Then, as today, Mitchell reels could always be relied on to do the job. Most prefer the 300 or 400 size, but in my eel-fishing days we used the larger 306 which held plenty of heavy line. I still have those reels and if I am bank fishing I use them today. A lot of nonsense is talked about reels these days and everyone is constantly changing reels for ones with more and more features. It is a pity that a lot of these reels rapidly fall to bits or prove otherwise unreliable. I'll stick to Mitchells, thanks!

For boat fishing there is only one choice and that is the multiplier. ABU have always been the market leaders for freshwater multiplier reels and I have been using the Ambassadeur 6000C for many years. You can load any breaking-strain of line onto them without problems, cast as far as you need and have the advantage of bite indication with the drag set lightly. With these reels, there is no need at all to mess about with elastic bands or line clips. Because the drag is audible, they are also ideal for trolling. It takes a little practice to get used to these reels, but once you have done so, it is as simple as using any other type of reel. Most multipliers are not cheap, but those produced by ABU are so well made they last for years and years: a good long-term investment.

LINE

This is another item that can be expensive or very cheap, depending on what sort of quality you are looking for. I use bulk spools and never anything other than Platil. Line is often a matter of personal choice, but it pays to stick with what you have confidence in. Platil is supple and is resistant to abrasion. It is not as fine in diameter as some lines, but for pike fishing this is of little importance. For all my general pike fishing I use Platil of 12 lb (5.5 kg) breaking-strain, but will happily step up to 15 lb (7 kg) when I am fishing waters such as Loch Lomond. Any situation that puts snags and weed between you and the fish calls for a heavier line. There are no rewards for losing pike and indeed it is quite possible that a lost fish is a dead fish in some circumstances. Another factor to bear in mind is line life. A good line will last for most of the season, particularly if you discard a few feet every few sessions, so as to ensure that the business end has not been hammered too hard. Constant stretching damages a line, so if you are doing very long-range casting it pays to change your line rather more frequently than you would otherwise.

Because pike have an impressive and powerful set of teeth, using nylon instead of wire is a false economy in that it will inevitably result in the fish biting through the trace. This is bad for everyone concerned, but particularly the pike. There are quite a few wires on the market these days, nearly all derived from American trolling wires. They are generally made from seven strands of wire and fairly stiff. They twist up well to make a trace and will last many trips, unless you happen to be catching fish one after the other. Traces should be 18–20 in (45–50 cm) long – certainly no shorter. My own preference has long been for Marlin Steel in 20 lb (9 kg) breaking-strain. It is pointless using finer wire because by doing so you are in effect removing the safety margin. Kinks and curls do appear in all wires and the stronger wire is less likely to snap if a fault occurs. There are several new wires now on the market, including some coated with Kevlar. I understand that they are kink-resistant and durable. If this is so, then there is a chance that some of the wires currently in use will become obsolete.

HOOKS

Hooks are fairly easily dealt with, simply because treble hooks in two sizes do the job for all of my pike fishing. Years ago, I started off by using single hooks and then a combination of singles and trebles. These seemed to work well enough, but eventually, as I started to require larger baits, my hooking success rate started to drop. It was the need to hook zander, a sometimes finicky feeder, that eventually pushed me into using treble hooks and since then I have never looked back. There are a number of makes of treble hooks and over the years I have used most of them. When Peter Drennan first moved into pike-fishing tackle I advised him on the right type of hooks and wire to use for making up ready-made pike traces.

A treble hook used for pike fishing has to be something of a compromise. It must be reasonably sharp, with either two barbless points or at least very small barbs, and it must also be strong enough to withstand considerable pressure. This is partly the reason why hooks smaller than size 10 are rarely used in pike fishing. Such small hooks are just not up to the job of holding on to very powerful fish. It is fairly easy to make a good strong hook in sizes 8 and 6 and Drennan have done very well with the range they sell. Another hook that I have used quite a lot is the Partridge outpoint, another good strong pattern.

Thickness of hooks

The reason most anglers lose fish is usually that the hook-hold fails or the angler has never really gained a proper hold in the first place. If the hook is made of fine wire, as are many of the round-bend patterns, the hooks are very sharp, yet the wire is simply not strong enough. It can then do two things: straighten out or snap. When a big pike comes up on to the surface of the water the violent thrashing is such that some hooks will snap or straighten. This is why you are better off with a hook made from thicker wire. You will lose little in hooking efficiency, but gain a lot of strength. There has been some intense debate over the years on the subject of barbless hooks, although really we should use the term 'semi-barbless'. The argument for semi-barbless trebles is that, by having only one bait-retaining barb and two hooks without barbs or with the barbs crushed flat, it is much easier to unhook the pike if by accident the hooks should end up deeply lodged.

The 'anti' argument says that if unhooking is made easier, then the pike must surely be able to unhook itself more easily. The theoretical argument also goes further, saying that if there is good cause to have confidence in semi-barbless hooks, then why not fish totally barbless. The opponents of semi-barbless hooks have missed the point, however. While it is true that these hooks will give a good hook-hold, providing some tension is kept on the line, it is also true that sometimes a slack line could cause the hooks to drop out. But in practice this is very rare, for after all we are supposed to be winding the fish in, not taking it for a walk! Situations where a pike is allowed slack line hardly ever occur. If reasonable weight is used to anchor the bait, the hooks will always be under some sort of tension. However, very little, if any, tension is kept on the bait itself and, particularly in the case of livebaits, it would be very easy for the bait to wriggle off. Hardly a fair comparison.

In fact, I and many other pike anglers have total confidence in semi-barbless hooks. So much so that I would happily fish against anyone fishing barbed hooks, but I would not enjoy helping to unhook any pike which swallows the bait. There is a school of thought that suggests that semi-barbless hooks, because they are more easily removed, lead to more delayed strikes and therefore more deeply hooked fish. The fact is, however, that if your gear is up to the job then an early strike will nearly always connect and if it does not, the fish was almost certainly small anyway.

There is not much to say about the really small items of tackle, except always avoid cheap products. Swivels, for example, can be bought from any tackle shop, but always go for one such as Mustad or Drennan, simply because they are of good quality and will not break when you least need it. Small-bore beads for stopping floats are now easily available. Once you had to buy cheap necklaces and got funny looks from sales staff in department stores! Stop-knots are made from black Dacron. This holds fairly tight, without causing line damage when you need to move the knot.

FLOATS

These are simplicity themselves: ET Polyballs serve as sunken pater-noster floats in black, while for surface fishing I use Polyballs painted fluorescent red with black undersides. Rarely do I use any other type of float, although in the old days we used to use 'Long Tom' floats, which were attached by the end ring only and gave excellent warning of a run when fishing on Fen drains. For drifting a bait out then I would use an ET 'Drifter' fished either end-ring-only, with a pilot float to keep the line up, or attached top and bottom.

I use shop-bought 1½–2 oz (45–60 g) leads, while SSG non-toxic shot is used when wobbling, trolling or ledgering deadbaits. Gener-ally, you will need six to a dozen traces ready for use. There is nothing worse than having to make up traces in the middle of intense action on a really cold day. It is far better to prepare them when things are quiet and it is a nice day. Traces can be held on a foam roll stored in a tin or you can use a ready-made strong version known as the 'Trace Tidy'.

Bite indicators

When boat fishing, bite indication is no problem since you can rely on the float or ratchet on the multiplier reel. For bank fishing, you can watch drop-off indicators and floats, which we had to do in the old days. However, this requires prolonged concentration and does not allow the angler any freedom of movement. By contrast, the use of buzzers enables tea to be brewed or allows the angler to concen-

The author seeking to improve his chances with three rods on a Loch Lomond bay.

trate on working one particular bait, safe in the knowledge that a run on another rod will be registered straight away.

Efgeeco 'Optonic' indicators are a well-established accessory. They can be used in many situations and you have to use a drop-off indicator with them. They can bleep a lot in the wind, particularly if you have failed to tighten up properly. If you can afford it, invest in some 'drop-off' alarms. There are quite a few models available and the best known is probably the 'Backbiter'. This registers both full-blooded runs and 'drop backs', enabling the angler to have lapses in concentration without the pike swallowing the bait too deeply. The Backbiter fitted with a Gardner line clip is probably the best option, simply because this clip is much more easily adjusted than any other on the market.

The only snag with audible alarms is that if you set them too loud everyone else knows you are catching fish. This may not be a good idea in these days of highly competitive pike angling. I tend to keep the volume down on my buzzers so that no one except me and the pike know that fish are coming out!

Weighing a Loch Lomond pike of about 15 lb (7 kg). It was taken in the middle of a hot afternoon on a ledgered livebait from 4 ft (1.2 m) of water.

Other equipment

My rod rests are in the main made by Bob Jackson. They are of aluminium, for lightness, with a tungsten tip, which means that they are probably worth more than the rest of my tackle put together! The heads are the simple push-on Efgeeco type. My rod holdall is simply a roll-up model made from a piece of canvas. With anglers like me around, it is a wonder that anyone buys the more expensive ready-made kind. In fact, with most of my fishing done from a boat nowadays, I carry the rods ready made-up, eliminating the need for a holdall in most situations.

Of much more importance is a good-quality weighing sling that also doubles as a useful means of carrying odd bits and pieces of tackle. I use the medium ET weighing sling, which is far better than some of the flimsy nylon ones which can easily allow the pike to slide out of the other end! For weighing the fish I use a standard pair of Avon scales, which in the old days could pose a problem. Then, these scales weighed up to 32 lb (14.5 kg), which meant that a very big fish would take them down to the limit. Fortunately, Avon now produce a version which weighs up to 40 lb (18 kg) – I should be so lucky as to need a bigger set of scales than that!

For unhooking pike, a pair of artery forceps is essential. Generally, the longer the better. They should be of good quality, simply because cheap ones do not last. Forceps have an advantage over pliers in that they can lock onto the hook, giving the angler a chance to move things around without fear of the hook having to be relocated. Forceps can also be clipped to your clothing so that they are always to hand. I find this particularly useful if a pike arrives at the edge of the boat and does not warrant being brought aboard. This is better for the pike and saves the angler time when they are feeding like mad. Some people have built up extensive tool-kits to enable them to unhook pike, but, if you hook your pike cleanly, forceps are all you will need. If you use semi-barbless trebles, even deeply located hooks are easily removed with forceps.

Photographing the catch

Once all the unhooking and weighing has been done, if the fish is a particularly good one the camera has to come out. To get good photographs requires a degree of preparation. Until recently pike were retained in carp sacks made from black nylon, perforated to allow a good throughflow of water. While I have had little trouble with sacks, the pike do sometimes get their teeth stuck in the material and this can be messy. ET tackle now do a very good cross between a sack and a keepnet known as a 'Pike Tube'. Made from nylon, this tube has supporting rings and offers the pike more space and less chance of tangling with its teeth. The tube is a little more bulky and not quite as easy to stow away. It is not much use for spreading on the ground as protection for the pike. The best option is to have a tube and a sack – then you are ready for anything!

My own photography kit goes with me everywhere. I use two Olympus cameras, although there are many makes available today. Reliability is worth far more than a lot of gimmicks. The more complex the camera is, the greater the chance of something going wrong. Both cameras, the OM-2n and OM-10, have an automatic metering system which leaves me free to concentrate on important points such as getting everything in the viewfinder. As well as a standard 50 mm lens, I also use a 28–70 mm zoom which gives me the option of wide-angle shots or tight framing for close-ups. Such a lens is ideal for pike anglers who do not wish to be cluttered up with too much photographic equipment.

When fishing alone it is essential to be able to take photographs by remote control. I have a small folding tripod and mount the camera on this after focusing on a couple of banksticks at the point where I will kneel with the fish. The banksticks can then be laid on the ground out of camera shot. An air bulb release is connected to the camera's shutter release and it is then a matter of kneeling on the bulb when ready. Most cameras have self-timers, but this does not give me the control of the air release. With the camera on a tripod it means that shutter speeds down to $\frac{1}{30}$ sec can be used without camera shake spoiling the picture. It is always a good idea to use as small an aperture as possible so as to increase the depth of field. Depth of field is the distance in front of the camera which is in focus. The smaller the aperture the greater the depth of field. However, the smaller the aperture the slower the shutter speed required for correct exposure and the greater the risk of camera shake.

Sometimes you need to compromise to obtain the best results and if light conditions are so poor that you cannot use a small aperture

The author with a fine trio of pike taken from Norfolk's River Bure. The largest weighed 23¼ lb (10.5 kg), the others 15 lb (7 kg).

you should use a flash instead. Automatic flash units are quite cheap and these provide the exact amount of illumination required. There are quite a few tricks employed by the professional photographer and these are best studied in a book on photography. However, if you stick to the basic simple rules you will get good photographs most of the time. Always take several pictures of each fish and it is often worthwhile taking pictures at aperture settings either side of the one suggested by the camera. To do this you will need a camera with a manual override. The problem with some highly automated cameras is that they do not give you this option.

Most photographers have their own favourite film. These days the reproduction of prints from slide film is very good, so there is little point in using colour print film for the photo-album work. Also, slides are much better for reproduction in magazines and news-papers. Black and white pictures can also be taken from slides and because of this I now use slide film most of the time. The speed of the film (ISO number) denotes the sensitivity of the film. The higher the number, the better it works in dull light. Unfortunately, the faster the film (the higher the ISO number), the more distinct is the 'grain' of the film. In simple terms, this means that a photograph taken on a fast film will not be of as good a quality when blown up to a large size as one taken on a slower film and enlarged. I generally opt for either ISO 64 Kodachrome or ISO 100 Fujichrome. Both are good-quality slide films and it pays to carry several around with you, for that day when things really work out.

Landing nets

The choice of landing nets is wide these days, but this was not always the case and my first net was a home-made one with a piece of copper pipe as the spreader. The net I use now was made by Steve Tolan and has a metal spreader and hollow glass-fibre arm and handle. This is very light and is well matched with a single-mesh knotless net. The arm is 42 in (1.1 m) long.

Pike anglers have to carry a lot of bait around with them and a good-sized bin is essential. These can be obtained for nothing if you know where to look. Frying-oil containers with a handle and a tight-fitting lid make ideal bait bins. They hold two or three gallons (9–15 litres) of water, ample for ten to twenty livebaits. Generally, in winter, not much aeration is needed when transporting the bait fish. When I arrive at my swim I simply cover the bin with a piece of netting and hold this on with an elastic strap. Submerged beside the boat or in the margins, the baits can be kept all day.

Deadbaits can be kept reasonably well frozen if wrapped up in newspaper, although on warm days it is better to use an Insulbag and a freezer block. For longer trips, a freezer box with lots of blocks is essential. Keep the box out of the sun and well covered, because most of those available these days are only lightly insulated.

I should also mention the additional items that either make for more comfortable fishing or enable me to fish areas inaccessible from the bank. I used to wear all sorts of makeshift fishing suits, mostly army surplus, and while they seemed good at the time, most were decidedly not waterproof. These days there is only one piece of clothing worth wearing and that is the Bob Church one-piece suit. You have only to look at the number in use on the river bank to realize that it is extremely popular and rightly so. The one-piece suit does away with the need to wear a top coat and leggings. It prevents the rain and wind getting in where it would have done between the two. When you are boat fishing it is particularly vital to keep warm and dry – otherwise the nagging thought of going home can become converted into action. That most neglected area, your bottom, also benefits by being totally waterproof. Like it or not, you are destined to sit on it for most of the day and once it gets wet, it is no fun at all. Waxproof suits such as Bob Church's breathe, avoiding condensation inside. This is a common problem with plastic suits.

There is plenty of choice of footwear these days. If you have to walk a long way then ordinary wellingtons or Derriboots are most useful. If not, you might opt for one of the brands of 'Moonboots'. I used to wear a pair of Doc Marten's boots for much of my fishing, for in many situations there is no real need to paddle around.

USING A BOAT

Not many anglers own a boat (see diagram on page 62), but when you consider the advantages of even a small inflatable it soon becomes clear that they are missing out. In the days when I fished the Delph a lot, an inflatable boat was essential for crossing the Old

Bedford to reach the Delph. The short boat crossing saved many miles of walking and this would probably have been impossible anyway, carrying all our fishing gear. Obviously a cheap inflatable is not the sort of boat to fish from, although one can be used to ferry gear out on to islands which cannot normally be fished from.

Inflatable boats

Avon make very seaworthy inflatables and a number of anglers use these for visiting waters where access is very poor. It is much easier to carry an Avon boat than a heavy glass-fibre one of the same size. Most people are nervous of inflatables, thinking that a set of hooks will puncture them, with those on board sent to a watery grave. Naturally, great care should be taken, and provided this is the case there should be no danger. Glass, wooden and aluminium boats are not expensive if bought secondhand and several keen pike anglers that I know have a couple of different sizes for different situations. I have used a variety of types of boat and each has plus and minus points. Wooden boats are heavy and hard work to maintain, yet they

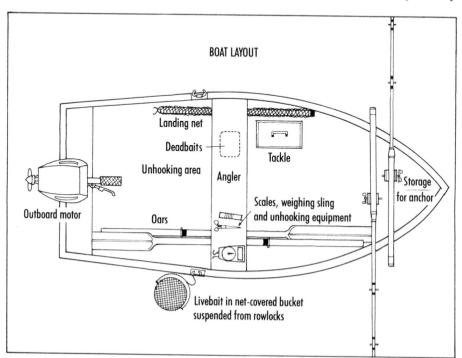

BOAT LAYOUT

Landing net

Deadbaits

Unhooking area

Tackle

Angler

Outboard motor

Scales, weighing sling and unhooking equipment

Oars

Storage for anchor

Livebait in net-covered bucket suspended from rowlocks

provide sound and stable platforms. They are fairly quiet to fish in, particularly once they have been lined with carpet or underlay. This floor covering is essential if you are boat fishing, since it protects the pike from knocks and bumps on the hard surfaces of the boat.

Most boats these days are made from glass-fibre or a combination of plastic and resin. The weight of the boat depends very much on the thickness of the material used. It is quite possible to make glass-fibre boats very light, but to do this the hull of the boat must be extremely thin. Thin hulls lead to the boat sitting very high in the water, to its being very susceptible to wind and, of course, a thin hull is more easily holed. The thicker-hulled boats are more difficult to launch in awkward situations, but in general they ride a lot better and are much more durable.

Most single-man boat fishing can be carried out from a nine- or ten-footer (2.5–3 m). If two of you are going to fish, then a 12–13 ft (3.5–4 m) boat is required. On big waters a boat of 16–17 ft (around 5 m) is essential to cope with the weather conditions likely to be encountered. In the vast majority of cases the larger boats will have

A dawn start to a day's pike fishing on a trout water. Many trout reservoirs hold pike, but a boat is needed to seek them out.

some form of built-in flotation. This may consist of polystyrene foam or a double-skinned hull filled with air. Care has to be taken with double-skinned boats because if an accident occurs and the space fills up with water, the result is a boat which will not float. Furthermore, if you have to take the boat out of the water, you will end up exhausting yourself in the attempt.

Additional equipment for a boat

There are a lot of additional items that you can buy for your boat, and it is particularly convenient to do so if you keep it on one particular water. There are some very comfortable swivel seats which can be imported from the USA and these are luxurious compared with sitting on a hard wooden seat. A cuddy or small cabin is another item that would be well worth investing in. Alas, I have not yet progressed to this standard of boat fishing, but some lucky anglers have already found the benefits of having a cabin.

Probably the most neglected, and yet indispensable, item of boat-fishing equipment is the anchor. There are two types: the simple mudweight and the proper hook-type anchor. For most pike fishing the mudweight is the most popular anchor. This is because most boat fishing is carried out with the boat directly above the anchors. A hook-type anchor only works really well when the boat is downwind of the anchor. Even this situation is not altogether satisfactory, because a long anchor rope allows the boat to sway around, which tends to make bite detection very difficult. Mudweights on short ropes, directly under the boat, are therefore preferred for most boat fishing in smaller waters.

The anchor's weight depends on the situation and your own physical strength. A 28 lb (13 kg) weight is about as much as most of us can lift from a fair depth, although in shallow waters with a hard bottom, the strong men among us could shift a 56 lb (25 kg) weight. But rather than give yourself a hernia, it is better to use several weights of say 20 lb (9 kg) on separate ropes for holding out in rough conditions. The boat obviously needs anchoring at both ends, so you may have to carry a lot of paint-tins full of concrete or lumps of scrap iron. Another makeshift anchor is a sack full of rocks or bricks. On some waters there will be a plentiful supply of stones or bricks, thus avoiding the need to carry a load of weight around.

Two handsome fish – 20½ lb (9 kg) and 25¼ lb (11.5 kg) – taken by the author on successive casts on drifted herring.

Secure anchorage

On very extensive waters a hook-type anchor will have to be employed and this is best backed up with 5–10 ft (1.5–3 m) of heavy chain, to help the anchor to grip. A hook-type anchor can be put out from the bow with a mudweight over the stern. If a good solid anchor of this type fails to hold out, then you would probably be better off on the bank! Anchor ropes should be fairly thick in order to avoid cutting into your hands. There are some very neat spring-loaded clips which allow anchor ropes to be secured easily and without fear of them coming undone. They also enable a quick release in an emergency. Cleats can also be attached to the boat, thus enabling the rope to be tied off at any particular depth.

The power for the boat can be as basic as a set of oars, in which case they should be in good condition, because it is no good if an oar breaks when you most need it. Rowlocks should be metal ones, tied in so that they cannot be lost. A good petrol-powered outboard motor is essential and there are plenty of these around. A 4 hp model can be picked up second hand for £100–200 or, if you can afford more, a new Yamaha 4 will cost about £450. For most work on English waters a motor of 4 hp is ample, though if you are out on the big waters a 6 hp model is better because it cuts travelling time considerably. Loch Lomond specialists who have very well-appointed boats now use outboard motors at least as powerful as this, which means that any area is within easy reach. However spending on this scale is only for the better-off angler!

Echo-sounders

An essential for any boat angler is an echo-sounder. I have used a Seafarer for a few years now and although it is only a basic model registering depths, if read properly it is of enormous help in finding the fish. It is now possible to buy much more sophisticated units, showing everything, including the fish. I recently brought a Hummingbird back from the USA. These LCD sonars have a screen which shows depth contours and will also pick up individual fish. There has been some debate about the use of such aids, but the problem remains even when you have found the fish: to get them to take your bait. If you are fishing a totally new water without any information, it can sometimes take many days to find fish. And when your holiday

Boat fishing in winter at Martham on Norfolk's River Thurne.

trip lasts only a week it is nice to have something that will help to put the odds a little more in your favour.

An LCD sonar costs about £200–400, but when you consider that an ordinary echo-sounder costs around £100, it is not much extra to pay for the additional information. Most echo-sounders will work off internal batteries, but they seem to devour them and it is therefore much better to use a 12-volt car battery. If you also have an electric trolling motor, then the purchase of a good-quality traction battery will enable you to run both from the same supply. Trolling motors are not generally of much use in Britain, simply because petrol motors are generally more powerful and last much longer. However, if you end up on a water where petrol motors are not allowed, a trolling motor can save a lot of rowing. From what I have said in this chapter it will be obvious that to fish seriously for pike takes a fair degree of organization and expense. Most committed pike anglers will invest in their sport so that they can increase their chances. The preparation does not stop on the river bank, however, for everything at home needs to be well organized, too. If possible, it is best to have a freezer specifically for the pike baits. In this way you do not end up finding that you have taken a pound of sausages to the water instead of the expected smelts!

Livebaits are the biggest problem for any pike angler and if getting them is difficult, so is keeping them alive. I either catch mine on rod and line or use simple wire-net traps for fish such as crucian carp. A big tank with ample aeration takes precedence over keeping the car in the garage and in this way I avoid having to worry about frozen tanks in the depths of winter.

CHAPTER FIVE

CATCHING PIKE

Pike fishing certainly offers the opportunity to use a wide variety of methods. I cannot think of any of the most sought-after coarse species which can be fished for on such a vast range of different waters and with such a variety of techniques. Before I describe individually the methods I and others use for catching pike, it will help to study the diagram on page 70 that shows the relationships between them.

First, it should be appreciated that much of pike fishing depends on presenting what is to the pike natural food. Live and dead fish are quite natural to pike, although of course the variety of fish, particularly of deadbaits, may be something that the pike would never expect to see. There are very few herrings swimming about in freshwater! Pike probably fail to appreciate the origins of a bait fish anyway, although they can distinguish the difference between certain species in some cases. There is nothing at all natural to the pike about wood, plastic, rubber or metal, yet a lure represents something edible, no matter how tenuous the connection might seem between it and natural food items. With other fish species – carp, for example – some of the baits used are totally alien and bear no relation at all to the usual diet. With pike, at least, we normally have the advantage of offering a bait similar to natural food.

LIVEBAITING

At present livebaiting is perhaps the most emotive issue in angling. This is mainly because of people looking around for something to get worked up about and others who think that if we give it up then the opponents of angling will pat us on the head and just go away. Neither the do-gooders nor angling's opponents seem to understand

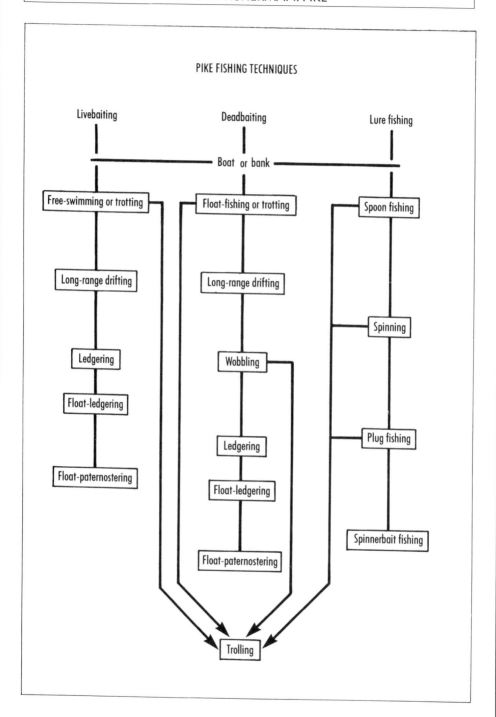

PIKE FISHING TECHNIQUES

that underwater it is like a jungle and that no quarter is given or asked for. Fish are there to eat and be eaten. All the pike angler who livebaits is doing is making it easier for the pike to catch its prey. When a pike catches a free-swimming fish it does not dispatch it immediately, thinking that this is the 'humane' way to carry on. The prey fish is grabbed, punctured by the pike's teeth and then swallowed alive. To us this might seem cruel, but in reality this is how animals behave and we can do nothing to change this. When a pike takes a livebait that is mounted on hooks, the same happens.

Quite a few ex-livebaiters have gone into print announcing that they have given it up, as if it is some terrible habit that they should never have allowed themselves to fall into. Of course, they have caught their big pike and made a name. Now they want to make sure that no one else can do the same. Make no mistake: in certain pike waters a livebait is the only consistent producer of big pike. To remove the option to livebait is on a par with removing the right to use maggots and worms. Yes, you can catch on bread and sweetcorn, but there are enough problems in angling without making it even harder with such restrictions.

Sadly, these days many clubs are banning the use of livebaits. They are happy to do so, because hardly any of the club members who support such a ban actually fish for pike. Some people say that livebaiting is cruel, but if that is so and we are so dedicated to protecting the rights of the individual roach, should we not kill the pike to stop the roach being eaten? When a pike takes a roach it does not attempt to kill it quickly. Banning livebaiting will not of course stop anglers using this method. All it will do is drive it underground and further alienate the pike angler from the rest of angling. My view is that if clubs impose livebait bans we should try, via the PAC, to make them change their minds. However, if this does not work, it is every man for himself and the decision to livebait or not remains with the individual. If you get caught you risk losing your club membership, so the golden rule is to not to get caught!

Livebaiting is also hard work, because you have to make considerable efforts to obtain and keep bait. Presentation of the bait is also more difficult, simply because livebaits do not stay still. It is understandable why some people cease to bother with livebaiting, but that does not invalidate the method as a catcher of larger numbers of pike

– and the big ones as well. Unless you are very lucky, the choice of livebait may well be a case of using what is available. For years I have made great use of species such as dace and crucian carp, although just about every species has been pressed into use at one time or another. Different fish have different swimming actions and, of course, different colours. I was convinced when fishing the River Delph that the darker, slower-moving crucians were better catchers of the really big pike than other baits. My results and those of others fishing with me confirmed this. A similar pattern prevailed on the Ouse when fishing perch livebaits.

If choice of species is not something you are blessed with, then at least a choice of size is likely to be. Ideal pike baits will be around 4 oz (110 g), with perhaps the odd one of up to 6 oz (170 g). A decent-sized bait offers the pike something worth chasing. A big pike is not going to get much joy out of a 1 oz (30 g) gudgeon, whereas a good-sized roach or crucian carp is an altogether different matter. However, limits on the size of livebait you can use are imposed by the difficulty in hooking the pike and the resentment shown by other, non-pike anglers.

Although a livebait is perhaps the most natural of pike baits, the moment it is tethered to a set of fishing tackle it ceases to behave in a natural manner. This is all very well on waters where pike have seldom been fished for or where the pike are hungry. However, on hard-fished waters or where prey fish are very numerous, subtle improvements in presentation can result in many more pike.

FREELINED LIVEBAIT

Possibly the most challenging method of presentation is the freelined livebait (see diagram opposite). Unfortunately it is not a method which lends itself to the relaxed approach. Casting a bait out and allowing it to swim around without weight or float causes considerable problems of bite detection, making it necessary to hold the line at all times. For most pike fishing this method is not really practical, but there are situations where it can be applied and these are invariably those where the pike are encountered at short range.

It sometimes happens that a pike will follow a livebait, wobbled deadbait or even a deadbait wound in backwards to the bank or

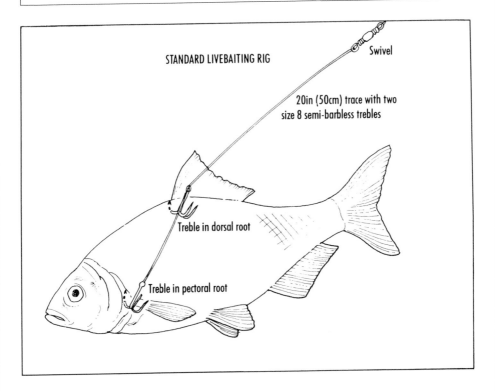

STANDARD LIVEBAITING RIG

Swivel

20in (50cm) trace with two
size 8 semi-barbless trebles

Treble in dorsal root

Treble in pectoral root

boat. Such pike will frequently be nervous and will seldom take a conventional bait, no matter how long you wait. The answer is a freelined livebait dropped in at the edge and allowed to swim around. Such a natural-looking bait quite often fools the pike lurking nearby and the take can be quite violent compared with the suspicious trailing of moments before. Another occurrence, albeit exceptional, that might prompt the use of a freelined bait is an abortive strike at a livebait fished paternoster style or float-fished. The float might be putting the pike off, in which case a free-swimming bait could make a difference.

A much more commonly employed technique is the simple float-fished livebait. This method can be used to cover a very large area of water and is of specific use when you are searching for the pike. It is also a fairly natural presentation of a livebait and with a little application a bait can be made to cover the water in a reasonably systematic manner. The tackle is very simple: just a streamlined float, a stop and a set of hooks. It helps if the line is greased and with some baits a certain amount of weight is required to keep the fish swimming well below the surface. When a bait of around 4 oz (110 g) is used, it is possible to get it to cover a large area of water.

The secret lies in the way the bait fish responds to resistance. Resistance is provided by the line making contact with the surface film and the float. The natural response of the bait fish is to swim away from this resistance. This means that a bait will, if checked, swim away from the angler. If the wind is blowing across the swim the bait will work upwind as far as it is able and may then drop downwind and start to swim upwind again when it has recovered. When there is a backwind the bait may be inclined to swim back towards the angler. Here, checking of the line can provide the required amount of resistance to get the bait to swim away. The advantage of getting the bait to swim off is that it avoids casting, for if this is done too many times, the result is a much less active bait.

The free-roving bait gives a lurking pike a fair chance of taking it, although it is sometimes after the bait has been through the swim several times that a take comes. The most effective baits for float fishing are those that are fairly active. Such baits include roach, dace and chub. Perch and crucian carp tend to spend more time trying to swim downwards, and so are less useful for searching out the water. However, if there is a strong breeze, the greased line will ensure that they cover a good area.

The float-fished livebait is a very useful method of presentation and many big pike have been caught in this way. Dennis Pye, for example, caught almost all his big pike using this technique in which, legend has it, he was particularly skilled. But float-fishing livebaits is just one method and the versatile pike angler will command a much wider range of techniques.

FREE-SWIMMING LIVEBAIT METHOD

The technique of using a free-swimming livebait is among the most exciting (see diagram opposite). Because you are always at work, the action only relents when you wind in for a break. A response from the pike can sometimes be a long time coming, yet the feeling of anticipation is always there. Such a feeling was well rewarded on a wild windy day in the 1970s while I was fishing the Old Bedford

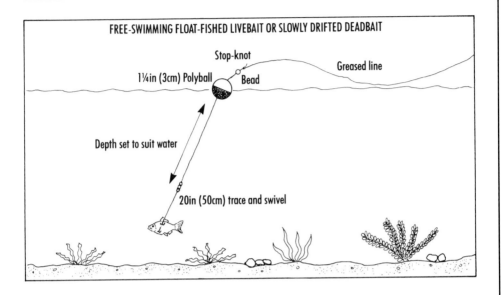

FREE-SWIMMING FLOAT-FISHED LIVEBAIT OR SLOWLY DRIFTED DEADBAIT

Stop-knot

Greased line

1¼in (3cm) Polyball   Bead

Depth set to suit water

20in (50cm) trace and swivel

Drain near Welney. I knew that the Bedford had produced pike of over 20 lb (9 kg) for some of my friends, and I was in the right area. However, despite covering a few hundred yards of water, nothing of note had happened. On this drain of around 20 yards (20 m) in width, my approach was to drift a large dace livebait along the drain, winding in and recasting, each time working a little farther along. By late afternoon the wind had risen to gale force and big 'rollers' were surging down the drain. Although these weather conditions might have been regarded as adverse on some waters, on this drain they allowed me to work the bait quite nicely along the far margins where the reed-lined edges might have been harbouring the odd big pike. Slowly, my enthusiasm was going. Then, as I went to lift the bait out from the margins, a big pike shot out and grabbed it. The fish weighed in at 21½ lb (10 kg) and was my biggest pike to date, and also my first from the Bedford.

The moral here was simple: if you cover a lot of water, there is always a chance. In fact my first-ever twenty-pounder (9 kg) from Vernatt's Drain fell to the same method, as did a string of other good fish. The free-swimming livebait is a particularly useful method for dropping a bait on the head of a pike which has shown on the surface. The assumption here is that a pike which shows itself is a pike which is active and likely to be looking for food.

Among the most exciting pike tactics is to fish a free-swimming livebait. The pike here was taken by this technique used from a boat.

A variation on the free-swimming float-fished bait is the trotted bait. On rivers the method can be used to search out the water. Here it is much better to be in a boat because this avoids the need for frequent casting and the associated problem of getting through a lot of baits. On slow-flowing rivers you are better off with smaller baits. You will struggle to get a larger bait to run downstream, for it will invariably swim against the flow. In faster-flowing rivers the current and drag on the terminal tackle and line will help to move everything downstream. When boat fishing it is quite easy to cover huge areas of water, simply by changing the position of the boat. In deep, fast-flowing rivers you may have to use a fair amount of weight to keep the bait down: around five or six SSG may be required. When the pike are feeding hard this approach can yield a large number of big fish and there are several fast-river specialists who have taken as many as ten pike of 10–20 lb (4.5–9 kg) in a day. This is hectic fishing by any standards.

DRIFTING FLOAT TECHNIQUE

A natural progression from float-fished baits is to add a drifting float and use this to cover a much larger area of water (see diagram on page 78). A variety of drifting floats are used these days. I use the ET 'Drifter'. This can be fished attached via the two rings top and bottom or, when fished by the end ring only, with a pilot float to keep the line on the surface.

The main purpose of the drifting float is to get a bait to areas which cannot be reached by conventional tactics. Drifting floats have been used in this way by a variety of anglers for many years, but the credit for popularizing the method must go to Eddy Turner, after whom his drifting float is named. Eddy and his friends found that while fishing big waters such as Abberton, in Essex, they could reach areas where baits were seldom presented. The result was a string of big fish, the best of which was a superb thirty-three pounder (15 kg). The boat angler, of course, does not have this problem of inaccessible areas, but it is not always possible to get a boat onto some waters. The angler confined to the bank may well have to consider using drifting techniques, particularly where fishing pressure is driving the pike out well away from the bank.

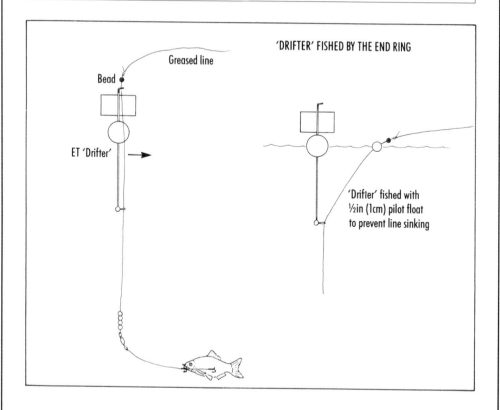

'DRIFTER' FISHED BY THE END RING

Greased line

Bead

ET 'Drifter'

'Drifter' fished with
½in (1cm) pilot float
to prevent line sinking

The technique of drifting requires a few modifications to the angler's normal set up. A livebait will usually move along at a fair rate while under a drifting float, and so it is best to fish it with its head facing up the trace. This also helps to avoid drowning the bait on the long wind-in back to the bank. The line has to be kept well greased and to do this it is possible to use a small attachment known as an 'autogreaser' that fits into the butt ring of the rod. You fill it with grease from time to time during the day and it keeps the line well greased and therefore floating on the surface. If the line sinks the float will not drift very well.

DRIFTED DEADBAIT

Deadbaits can also be fished under a drifting float and this tactic accounted for some very big fish at Llandegfedd, where livebaiting was not allowed. Generally, a good backwind is needed to get a bait to drift a long way out, but often the first few yards of water are fairly calm. If so, it may be necessary to cast the float and bait out. This has to be done with care because most of the vanes on drifting floats are fairly fragile. Another trick is to attach a balloon with a paper clip to the drifting float to give the wind something extra to push against. A gentle strike will release the balloon.

Once a bait is a long way out, perhaps as far as 150 yards (140 m), if you have plenty of bank space it is then possible to make the float drift along the bank at your chosen range. A huge area of water can be searched out with this method. The biggest problem with drifting is keeping the float in sight. This demands total concentration and cannot be done while you are watching several other rods. When a run does come, you should wind down until you can wind no more, then pull hard into the fish. No amount of frantic striking will hook a pike at long range, simply because the stretch in the line cancels out such efforts. By winding down tight you take the stretch out of the line as you wind and then, by a combination of pressure from the rod and resistance from the line and tackle, the pike is hooked.

The speed at which a bait drifts can be varied in a number of ways. Probably the easiest way is to vary the size of the vanes. These are easily interchanged and can be cut down to give the required speed of drift. An extra-large vane could be used when there is less wind. A bait can also be checked by allowing the line to be paid out by hand from the reel. This will cause the bait to move up and down to some extent in the water. The change in motion of the bait serves to wake it up and can also stimulate a pike that is following to attack it.

Methods that involve a moving bait are fine if pike are willing to attack the bait after only a brief look at it. However, this is not always the case and then a more static method of presentation has to be employed. This brings us to the method that still catches the majority of pike in Britain.

THE FLOAT-PATERNOSTER

In the past the float-paternoster rig tended to be somewhat crude and incorporated a lot of metalwork. The modern float-paternoster takes many, more refined, forms, but the basic principle remains the same: it presents a lively bait in such a way that its movements are limited to the area the angler puts it in. This serves a number of purposes. First, in rivers or waters with a strong undertow, it enables a bait to be kept where the angler thinks the pike are. Secondly, it gives a pike plenty of time to become aware that there is a 'free' meal in the area. Pike do not always take a bait straight away and the static paternoster rig allows plenty of time for a pike to decide whether or not to attack the bait. Another advantage is that it allows the angler to fish a bait near to snags or weedbeds without the fear of the bait going where it should not go. The rig also reduces the number of casts required to fish a particular swim and in so doing cuts the number of bait fish required for a session.

The basic float-paternoster came back into general use in the mid 1960s, when anglers such as Barrie Rickards, Ray Webb and Dave Steuart proved what a deadly method it could be in the right hands. Their approach was simple and I shall refer to it as the standard paternoster rig. The float can be used either on the surface or below it, and has often been a round one derived from the old pilot float. These days a 'poly ball' serves the same purpose. It used to be considered, with a surface-fished float, that the paternoster weight should be kept to the minimum in order to avoid creating resistance to the taking pike. Leads of only ½ oz (15 g) would be used and these would tend to keep the rig in place on a calm day. But it has since been realized that pike are not generally averse to dragging a big weight around with them and, in my opinion, a heavy paternoster weight both induces a pike to run with a bait and gives a much more positive bite registration.

The standard paternoster rig

Nowadays, the standard paternoster, like all the other such rigs, uses around 2 oz (60 g) of lead to hold a bait in position. This ensures that a tight line can be kept to a bait when either boat fishing or fishing from the bank with a drop-off bite indicator. The rig is simple, with either a three-way or two-way swivel used as the pivotal point. The trace, reel line and paternoster link all come from this central point.

In general, the longer the paternoster tail, the greater the bait's area of movement. However, since it is very difficult to present a bait on a tail longer than 4 ft (1.2 m), it is generally kept to around

Top Looking north on Loch Lomond towards Ben Lomond.
Above The author fishing the Waveney after a heavy frost.

At 23¼ lb (10.5 kg), this was the author's first pike of over 20 lb. It was taken on a paternostered live roach in January 1981.

As dawn approaches, two pikers are already on their way to a session on the Waveney near Beccles in Suffolk.

With his dog Sally by his side, the author shows off a fine 20 lb (9 kg) pike taken from a Fenland drain.

The author's first 30 lb plus (14 kg) pike, taken on a paternostered roach livebait at dusk on Norfolk's Decoy Broad in February 1981.

3 ft (0.9 m). A paternoster tail of this length also presents the bait well off the bottom, and the length can be varied during the day so that the bait can be fished between a limited range of depths. It is also possible to fish a bait near the surface of deep water, by coiling an extra-long paternoster link and holding the coils together with PVA string which dissolves when the rig hits the water. The result is that the link uncoils (in most cases) and the bait works more or less at any depth you want.

Problems with the paternoster

The snags with the standard paternoster are that to a certain degree it limits bait movement and it is also prone to tangles when used with hyperactive baits such as rudd and trout. While it is true that such problems can be countered by frequent inspection of the bait, it is also true that the repeated casting that this entails tends to reduce one of the advantages of the rig. The answer to this problem is to fish the same rig with an uptrace. This is in effect another wire trace above the swivel which serves to prevent 'bite-offs': when the bait gets above the swivel and becomes wrapped around the line. For all those who still prefer the standard paternoster, this rig is still probably the best adaptation of it.

Another way of overcoming problems is to attach the paternoster link halfway along the wire trace using a sliding-float stop knot. This serves a similar purpose to the uptrace in that baits seldom manage to get themselves around the reel line. However, this method, along with that of attaching the paternoster link directly to the hooks, restricts bait movement so much that I consider it to be a big disadvantage when livebaiting and best used with deadbaits. After all, what is the point of fishing with something which is supposed to attract pike by its movement, if you then allow the whole lot to become tied up in knots?

A slightly more flexible method involves making the paternoster tail a running one, so that a bait can pull line through the paternoster link swivel. This does allow increased movement of the bait, but in its original form it presents the same risk of the bait finding the reel line as the standard paternoster does. There are ways around this problem, but there are also other alternatives which make further experimentation unnecessary.

Trouble-shooting paternoster rig

My own version of the paternoster solves all the problems that I have come across and also, in my view, presents the bait to its best advantage. Again, the Polyball is used and is usually a dark colour and fished sunken. The line runs through the float, and carries a small-bore bead to enable the stop-knot to set the float at the predetermined depth. The reel line ends at a swivel, from which the paternoster link continues to the bomb. All paternoster links are of a lighter breaking-strain than the reel line. In this way if the link does get snagged, the bomb will be lost rather than the reel line breaking, which can only lead to the loss of the fish.

The main difference between my rig and the others is that the trace is free to run on the line. In this way the bait has a considerable degree of freedom. There are, of course, limits to this freedom and it may not be very useful to have bait swimming below the surface in 20 ft (6 m) of water. Therefore I use a simple stop made from a matchstick and valve rubber fitted on the line. I can limit the movement of the bait, within the depth band I feel is most likely to produce pike. Provided the line is kept tight, this rig stays remarkably tangle-free and has been responsible for a lot of my big pike. Probably the most significant of these was a fish of 31¼lb (14 kg) caught from Decoy Broad just as it got dark – my first pike over 30 lb (14 kg). I will never forget the big hole in the water which appeared just after that particular fish took the bait!

Some fellow anglers have expressed surprise about my fishing sunken paternosters from a boat, but there really is no problem in doing so. With the multiplier set for bite indication, the slightest movement of the bait will register. Even slack-line takes are easily spotted, provided you are watching your rod top, even if this is unfashionable these days!

There are so many difficulties facing the pike angler that good presentation of lively baits can prove crucial. The paternostered livebait technique presents a bait in such a way that a pike is actually encouraged to take it. If you had a bar of chocolate suspended in front of your nose for three hours there would be a good chance that eventually you would try to eat it, even if you had just eaten a good meal. It is this combination of greed and curiosity that we pike anglers work on!

Alternative paternosters

There are currently available a number of other paternosters which I do not use, but which are nevertheless worth a mention. There are, for example, various versions of Vic Bellar's or Colin Dyson's paternosters. In all these rigs the bait runs on the line above the float and lead. When you are using a tight line the bait can swim around in much the same way as with my rig, but once it is taken the lead is not towed around. This sort of rig might in odd situations be an advantage, although I cannot see the application to my style of fishing. It does present a very lively bait to advantage, but is not a good rig for casting, compared with the others.

A final paternoster variation is the one recently brought into use by Neville Fickling. This employs a piece of boom tube to protect the line and prevent 'bite-offs'. It is a little bit obvious, although whether or not this worries pike I am not sure. It is said to be almost tangle-proof, but I have heard that said about all rigs.

The biggest single disadvantage of the float paternoster is seen on very hard-fished waters. Pike will get very nervous of a bait which moves in an erratic manner. If you consider it, a paternostered livebait is in fact erratic and rather unnatural. On normal waters where the pike see only a few baits a season, the method will always work well. However, when the pike are hammered week in week out, presentation can become very important. Some might say that if the water is overfished, the angler should move to another, and to some extent I agree with this. However, many anglers do not have the luxury of changing venue, particularly in some industrial areas.

LEDGERED LIVEBAIT

If you suspect the paternoster is failing to work as well as it might, try a different method of presentation. I have already mentioned the float-fished and freelined livebaits and these do have a use in situations where the pike are nervous. However, it helps to have a static method in your repertoire to solve the problem of dour pike. The ledgered or float-ledgered livebait has a totally different action from the paternostered bait and as well as being effective in its own right, can sometimes prove to be a first-class alternative.

The rig is simplicity itself, with a reasonably large bomb used to

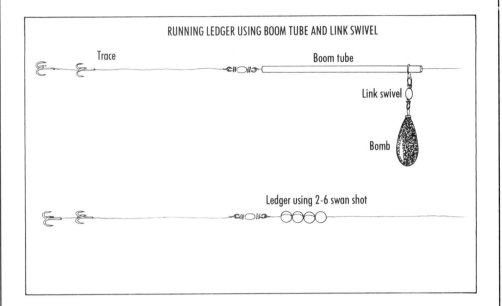

RUNNING LEDGER USING BOOM TUBE AND LINK SWIVEL

Trace

Boom tube

Link swivel

Bomb

Ledger using 2-6 swan shot

hold everything on the bottom (see diagram above). The livebait can be hooked head-up or tail-down, giving a slightly different action in each case. The longer the distance between bait and bomb, the greater the movement. Baits such as dace and rudd which tend to seek the surface are ideal for fishing in this manner.

Probably my best experience with ledgered livebaits came in the famous pike bay at Ardlui on Loch Lomond. Those anglers who have fished the bay will know that it is generally around 6 ft (2 m) deep, with areas of heavy weed cover. The bay can get very busy and you do not always get a choice of swim, as was the case on this trip, with Ken Hume and myself squeezing in where we could. My swim was weedy more than 15 yards (13 m) out, which left a small area of water some 3 ft (1 m) between me and the weed. It was the sort of area that was almost too shallow for a paternoster, so I opted for ledgered livebaits, reasoning that anything that passed through this area would be bound to see my bait.

Initially, no one caught much, but this was no reason for abandoning the plan. By early afternoon things had picked up considerably, and we had landed three fish to 10 lb (4.5 kg). Because it was quite hot it did not look as if much more would happen until later on. No doubt the pike were holed up in the weeds.

This 14¼ lb (6.5 kg) pike was taken on ledgered livebait by the author from Loch Lomond's Ardlui Bay.

At 8.30 pm the ledgered roach was taken by something which appeared to be in a great hurry. I hit it quickly, but it had already reached the weedbed. Luckily the weed was soft and it was easy enough to extract it. The pike weighed 22 lb 2 oz (10 kg), a personal best and my first over 20 lb (9 kg) from Lomond. It would soon be dark, but I put out another ledgered livebait anyway. When my next run came I was well and truly wound-up. This fish was an angry animal and the fight lasted at least five minutes before Ken managed to net it. Another personal best at 24 lb 8 oz (11 kg). In the following weeks as we made repeated visits, two more twenty-pounders (9 kg) were added to my score, proving beyond doubt that, in shallow water where the pike want a livebait, ledgering takes some beating.

If you look through the angling press you will see each week that many big pike are caught on deadbaits. There is little doubt that pike of all sizes will take advantage of an easy free meal. Yet it was not until recently in pike-fishing history that deadbaits were thought to be worth using. You can fish a deadbait with very little effort, but to do it properly takes just as much concentration as any other method.

86

The simplest of the static techniques is the simple freeline method with no weight on the line – just the weight of the bait. I avoid this approach, simply because the lack of resistance encourages finicky takes and this can lead to deep hooking owing to the pike's refusal to run with the bait. It is far better to put some weight on the line just above the trace. For fishing on the smaller Fenland drains, where flow is not often a problem, four SSG shot will allow the line to be tightened nicely. A drop-off indicator will then register the slightest movement of the bait.

FLOAT-LEDGERING

For most of my deadbaiting I prefer the float-ledger (see diagram on page 88). A Polyball is used and this is set several feet overdepth, so that the bait sits on the bottom. Four SSG shot will hold the rig in position nicely, unless there is a flow or undertow. In this case I add enough shot to keep things in place. The advantage of the float-ledger method is that it keeps the line out of snags and in shallow water helps to avoid pike swimming into the line with disastrous consequences. Provided you have the bait well anchored on the bottom, it is easy enough to keep the line tight, using a drop-off indicator while bank fishing or the drag on the reel while boat fishing.

The Polyballs I use are the ET type and are painted half orange and half black. Any early indications of a run usually entail the lifting of the float to show the black underside. Even on a windy day, this will be obvious if you are watching your tackle. I used to employ a variety of home-made floats for deadbaiting, and end-ring-only sliding floats which are cocked when the line is under tension work really well, either sliding away or keeling over when a pike picks the bait up. These days, because I do a lot of boat fishing, I seldom use these floats, since the odd swaying of the boat tends to make them tilt, giving false warnings of imminent runs.

Although much of my deadbaiting is static, I am a great believer in working the bait back to me while fishing a swim. This serves to put it somewhere near to a fish on those days when a pike is less inclined to move around. Another trick I like to use with deadbaits is to make them stand up off the bottom by means of a small piece of poly-

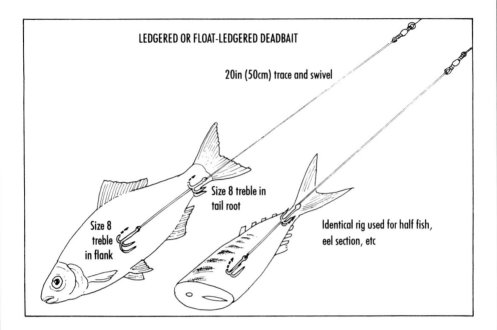

LEDGERED OR FLOAT-LEDGERED DEADBAIT

20in (50cm) trace and swivel

Size 8 treble in tail root

Size 8 treble in flank

Identical rig used for half fish, eel section, etc

styrene or balsa wood inserted in the bait's mouth (see diagram on page 90). This serves several purposes, including keeping the bait clear of bottom weed and helping to make it much more visible to the passing pike. While it is true that a half mackerel standing up on the bed of a lake is not at all natural, it is hardly more unnatural than a half mackerel in freshwater anyway. When you are fishing the same waters as other anglers it pays to offer something a little different. Buoyant baits are just this and I have every confidence that they will outfish most other presentations.

An approach that paid off

Possibly my most exciting catch with this method came at Martham Broad during the early 1980s, a time when poaching was the norm rather than the exception. The first trips were being made during the first year that a warden was working properly. I had previously been out at night with John Holliman and he had caught a twenty-four pounder (11 kg). On the next trip I went on my own because John could not make it. After mooring up against the reeds I put out a float-ledgered mackerel tail on one rod and a smelt on the other. Both baits were standing up off the bottom.

I had only been there thirty-five minutes when the reel gave a couple of clicks. I quickly wound down and hit the fish. In fact, the pike had run towards me, leaving a lot of slack line to be recovered. When I did make contact with the fish, much of the initial fight was on the surface, which was to be expected in such shallow water. Although I was fishing in the dark, not far from a big bed of reeds, I kept cool, knowing that provided I kept the pike away from those there would be no problem. But it decided it was going to get under the boat instead, although luckily it came out from there too.

When finally I had the fish ready for the net, I made a big mistake. I tried to use the small torch to help me guide the fish into the net. The pike promptly went berserk! Fortunately, at the next attempt I did better. The fish weighed in at 31 lb 10 oz (14.5 kg) and was my second and biggest fish over 30 lb (14 kg) and my first of this size to a deadbait – in this case a half mackerel.

One of the greatest advantages of deadbaits is their smell. I do not doubt that livebaits also have an odour that can be detected by pike. But a deadbait, particularly cut in half or punctured, must give off a scent trail that pike can home in on. In flowing water this must help pike to locate a bait, and in fact few waters are really still, since there is always some water movement due to current or wind. There are now a number of boosters available which can be injected into your deadbaits. Although it is a little too early to say for sure whether or not they work, anything that increases the smell of the bait and helps a pike find it must be worth trying.

SUSPENDED DEADBAIT METHOD

Although float-ledgering or straight ledgering are the most often used methods of deadbaiting, another static technique is also worth trying. This is the suspended deadbait, fished either on a float-paternoster or drifted around under a float. The method is seen by some anglers as being the lazy version of livebaiting: the angler cannot be bothered to catch the livebaits, therefore anything dead is substituted. Convenience is not always the motivation, however, for the suspended deadbait can be a very deadly method in its own right. On Fen drains and certain of the Norfolk Broads it can actually outfish a livebait.

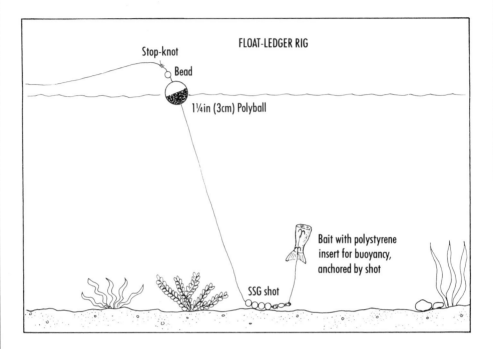

FLOAT-LEDGER RIG

Stop-knot

Bead

1¼in (3cm) Polyball

Bait with polystyrene insert for buoyancy, anchored by shot

SSG shot

There are two main theories as to why this method should be so successful. The first is the idea that a state of suspension and apparent lifelessness is almost natural behaviour for some fish species. The other theory is that the pike is not really interested in what the bait looks like; it thinks it is food and that is all it needs to know. I subscribe to both views, but appreciate that pike, because they are opportunist feeders, will feed on anything provided it looks edible and is not obviously attached to anything dangerous.

With the suspended-deadbait technique, it does not seem to matter one iota whether the bait is fished horizontally, vertically or head-down – pike will take it regardless. So for ease of casting it is just as well to cast the bait head-down, since in this way fewer baits fly off the hooks on the cast.

MOBILE DEADBAITING

You can drift or trot a deadbait just as you would a livebait. However, the most often used mobile technique is the wobbled deadbait. A few years back, pike anglers such as Fred Wagstaffe, Bill Keal and

The simplest rig for wobbling a deadbait: one treble hook is set in the mouth, the other in the flank.

Jim Gibbinson were doing very little but wobbling deadbaits (see diagram below). These days, when it is usual to sit behind a row of motionless rods, it seems to have gone out of fashion. Yet pike anglers in the know are still catching big pike on wobbled deadbaits. The method can be adapted to suit almost any water, weather conditions, or mood the pike are in. In its simplest form it consists of casting out a deadbait and winding it in. The movement gives the bait a degree of life.

The simplest wobbling rig is the standard set of two trebles. The top hook is fixed into the bait's mouth, while the bottom hook is inserted into the flank. By adjusting the position of the bottom hook, a degree of bend in the bait's body can be obtained. The greater the bend, the more pronounced the degree of wobble. With the bait's body at almost a right angle, a very pronounced revolving action can be obtained. The gentler the bend, the less the tendency of the bait to revolve. The right choice depends very much on the water being fished and the mood of the pike.

The amount of weight on the line and the type of bait will influence whether the bait fishes sub-surface or deep. Sea-fish baits such as sprats, sardines and herrings tend to sink and require little weight to get them to operate at any depth you choose. It is simply a case of letting the bait sink and then working it back slowly. Natural baits such as dead coarse fish and to some extent smelts, tend to float because the swim-bladder is intact. This can be an advantage, particularly if you wish to fish a bait on leadless tackle in very shallow

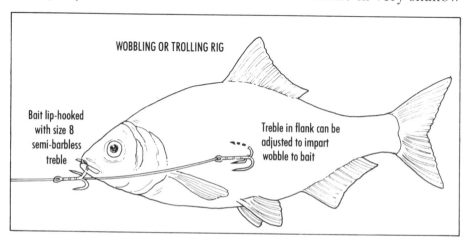

WOBBLING OR TROLLING RIG

Bait lip-hooked
with size 8
semi-barbless
treble

Treble in flank can be
adjusted to impart
wobble to bait

water or over weedbeds. Otherwise the swim-bladder can be punctured and the bait used in the same way as sea-fish baits.

Added buoyancy

It is an unfortunate fact that most sea baits are rather soft and therefore tend to split after a number of casts. For this reason, species such as roach and smelts again tend to make much better wobbling baits. However, repeated casting can deflate the swim-bladder and then, when fishing weedy water in particular, it is helpful to use a polystyrene or balsa insert. (For fishing deep waters there is a useful device marketed by Marvic tackle known as the wobbling pin. Weight can be added to the pin and this is then pushed down the bait's throat in much the same way as the insert.) In this way the bait will float until it either falls to bits or is taken. Another advantage of the bait's buoyancy is that after a pike has taken the bait and, as so often happens, throws it out, the bait of course floats and may be reused. If your baits have become a bit soft, which does happen with frozen coarse-fish baits, you can reinforce them by tying them up with elasticated thread. They are then less likely to come off during casting.

Wobbling is without doubt one of the most exciting methods in common use. Sub-surface fishing provokes a quite spectacular take from some pike. It is not unusual to see a big bow wave come up behind the bait as a large pike heads towards it, intent on chomping it. But life is not always as simple, and sometimes a pike will follow a bait without taking it. If you are wearing polarized glasses you will see the pike and can respond accordingly. If you are bank fishing, you will need to use whatever bankside cover is available. If you do not, the pike will see you and depart much faster than it arrived. When boat fishing you can only hope that the pike does not notice you and try not to make any sudden moves.

A standard trick introduced into Britain from the USA is the 'figure-of-eight'. This simply involves using the rod top to work the bait around in front of you in a figure-of-eight. It works very well with 'muskies' and sometimes fools the odd pike! An alternative approach is to let the bait sink in the hope that the pike will pick it up once it is sitting on the bottom. If this does not work, wind in and recast. The bait can then be worked back at a different speed. This is sometimes surprisingly effective. On rivers it is a good idea to move up- or downstream and cover the same area from a different position. Whether the bait is being worked up- or downstream can greatly influence how a pike reacts to it. If all else fails, drop a free-swimming livebait near to where the pike was last seen. Wobbling may not always catch the fish, but if you are quick enough to follow on with another method such as that just mentioned, you can snatch victory from the jaws of defeat.

LURE FISHING

Wobbling is in many ways akin to lure fishing (see diagram below). The debate continues as to whether pike think that lures are fish or simply take them out of curiosity or anger. But one thing is certain: the pike angler who ignores lures will miss out on a lot of fun and sometimes a big fish or two. There are so many lures available

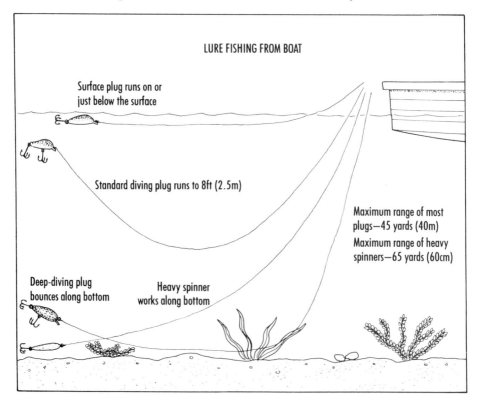

LURE FISHING FROM BOAT

Surface plug runs on or just below the surface

Standard diving plug runs to 8ft (2.5m)

Maximum range of most plugs—45 yards (40m)

Maximum range of heavy spinners—65 yards (60cm)

Deep-diving plug bounces along bottom

Heavy spinner works along bottom

nowadays that many anglers measure their lure-fishing prowess by the number of lures they have in their box. But what is the point of buying a lot of weird and wonderful creations if you never use them? A basic range of tried and tested lures will always catch pike that are responsive to lures.

Long before American lures were easily obtained in Britain, ABU were about the only firm selling really good-quality plugs and spoons. The Hi-Lo is an interesting plug evolved from the Heddon River Runt. However, the Hi-Lo has the advantage of an adjustable diving vane, making it much more adaptable. It comes in a variety of sizes in either a single- or double-jointed version. The quality of these plugs remains unsurpassed and this is what counts if you want to land the pike you manage to hook.

Recommended patterns

Generally I opt for lures around 3–4 in (75–100 mm) long and in the more natural patterns such as that imitating perch scales. I have more confidence in lures that look like the natural prey, although plenty of other anglers have caught good pike on all sorts of garish creations. If you are a confirmed lure-fishing freak, it is possible to ring the changes by choosing from the vast variety of colours, but because I tend to use other methods as well, I do not generally get the time to try every colour in the range.

Creek Chub Pikie lures have also gained a well-deserved reputation over the years, and various models are now available, ranging from shallow runners to deep divers. The only problem with these imported lures is their extremely high price.

My first Broadland pike succumbed to a size 6 Swim Whizz plug and was taken from a corner of Wroxham Broad. The Swim Whizz is a shallow-diving plug with a lazy, side-to-side action. It is not possible to cast it a long way, but it is ideal for short-range work on narrow drains and in tight areas on broads.

Another lure for shorter-range work is the ABU Killer, which is basically a version of the Finnish Rapala. These long, thin lures have a very dramatic wobble when wound in fast, yet still wriggle attractively at very low speeds. It is generally rare, in the area I fish, to have to use any plug which dives deeply. Most Broadland waters are fairly shallow, eliminating the need for anything that goes down further than 10 ft (3 m). In many waters it is not vital to fish deep anyway: a pike that wants a lure will quite happily move up through the water column to hit a lure. Some lures produce a lot of vibration, and there is little doubt that a pike is well aware of such a lure even if it cannot see it. Many of the best-known pike lures have a built-in rattle, which obviously makes them noisier. As far as we know, pike have three senses: sight, sound and smell. Most lures depend on sight and sound for a reaction. The sight factor may be limited in many waters because of turbidity, but provided the plug makes plenty of noise it should be possible for the pike to be drawn near enough to see it. The fish can then make its final decision. A number of lures are being introduced into Britain with an added smell factor, so that all the pike's senses are now catered for.

SPOONS

Plugs are not the only lures available to the pike angler. There are also a number of spinning or spoon baits. Perhaps the most famous of all, yet the most underrated, is the humble Toby Spoon. ABU make several versions of this spoon, the largest being the Salmo at 1¼ oz (35 g). The most commonly used size is the standard ⅝ oz (18 g) or the heavyweight 1 oz (30 g). All the Tobys cast really well and are ideal for searching out pike in large areas of water. They can be worked back fairly slowly, although the 1 oz (30 g) model does tend to seek out the snags if you are not careful. Pike will hit a Toby even if it is going fairly fast. The trick is to fish it as slowly as possible, but not allowing it to snag up. There is no point in losing a stack of lures or winding in weed every time!

Home-made spoons are also worth a try and it is not difficult to beat out some effective patterns from various gauges of copper sheet. All that is needed is a pair of tin-snips and a ball hammer. Some spoon makers have a wooden pattern on which the spoon is formed. Others simply beat away until the desired shape is obtained. All that is then required is to fit good-quality split rings, hooks and swivels. A useful extra for your tackle box is metal polish. Copper soon tarnishes and although there may be days when a dull spoon will score, it is best to have the option of giving the spoon a shine when required. I have seen some very good copies of the old

A prime example of what Norfolk's River Thurne can produce: a 28¼ lb (13 kg) taken by Alison Craig on a float-ledgered herring.

Above A small selection of plugs: surface runners, shallow runners, and divers.
Top right A small pike found this jointed surface plug irresistible.
Right Sally, attentive as ever, watches the author's struggle with a hard-fighting
summer pike of about 15 lb (7 kg).

A deadbait, clearly visible, is carefully removed with a pair of forceps, which make unhooking both easier and safer.

A 21 lb (9.5 kg) pike that succumbed to a Shakespeare 'Big S' plug on the River Bure at Wroxham in Norfolk.

Efgeeco Piker spoon and the real enthusiast will come up with many other patterns. You can even get your lures chrome-plated.

Commercially-made spoons are now much more easily obtained than they were a few years ago. Now that lure fishing has become popular again, the choice has increased tremendously. The Professor spoon from Finland has proved itself over and over again. It comes in a variety of sizes and colours, but it is generally the copper colour in the 4–5 in (100–125 mm) sizes that catches the fish. There are also available a few 'weedless' spoons which help the angler to fish in weed with less likelihood of snagging up. Some of these lures can also prove to be fishless lures if you are not skilful!

Spinnerbaits

The latest trend is the use of what are known as 'spinnerbaits', which are imported from the USA. They have proved highly effective in Britain. Each spinnerbait consists of two wire arms, on the end of one of which there are a hook and lead combined, these being neatly disguised by a plastic skirt or streamer. On the other arm are one or two spoon blades, which revolve as the lure is trailed through the water. The blades and streamer provide the attraction and the hook-and-weight combination focuses the pike's attention.

The hook is generally a large single, which leads to some fish being missed. When pike are missed in numbers, a stinger hook can be attached to the single. This is a treble fitted over the bend of the hook and held on with a piece of rubber tubing. Its addition helps the spinnerbait avoid getting snagged in weeds and this is one of this lure's big advantages. The single hook, being mounted point up, tends to bounce over snags and miss much of the weed that a conventional lure would pick up.

Spinnerbaits come in a range of sizes, but generally the ⅝ oz (18 g) or ½ oz (15 g) size are preferred. There are numerous types with all sorts of blades and colours of streamer, but a good choice to start with is one with a single copper blade and a red streamer. These can be fished 'sink and draw' – allowed to sink, retrieved for a few yards, and then allowed to sink again. Or they can be wound in with a steady winding action. It sometimes takes the odd jerk on the rod tip to keep them going at very slow speeds. They can also be fished quite fast just below the surface and, as with any surface fishing, the take can be spectacular.

Spinners

I suppose most anglers have thrown a spinner around from time to time. These are the lures with a blade that revolves around a central body. ABU in particular make a wide range and, like most good things, they are underrated. Yet each year anglers with minimal skill land some very big pike on them. With the upswing in interest in lure fishing, one or two anglers are looking again at spinners as pike-catchers. Again the variety is endless, but it does pay to start with the modest-sized patterns, as the really big ones probably frighten the pike rather than stimulate them.

Many other kinds of lure could have been mentioned, particularly surface plugs. However, there are anglers who are more experienced than me in their use and I would recommend reading what, for example, Barrie Rickards or Gord Burton have to say.

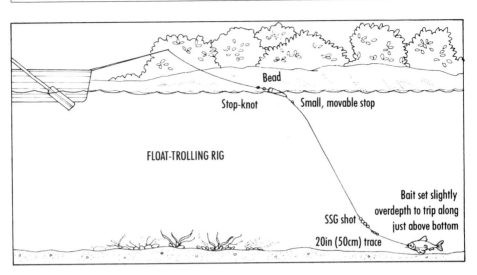

FLOAT-TROLLING RIG

Bead

Stop-knot

Small, movable stop

Bait set slightly
overdepth to trip along
just above bottom

SSG shot

20in (50cm) trace

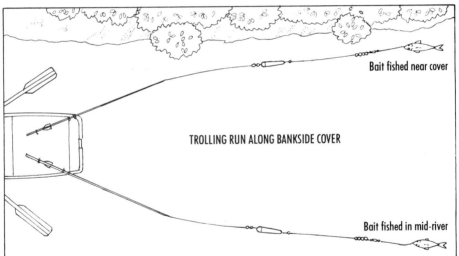

Bait fished near cover

TROLLING RUN ALONG BANKSIDE COVER

Bait fished in mid-river

FLOAT TROLLING

One final mobile technique does not fit into any clearly defined category, tending to draw from a range of disciplines according to the type of water being fished. This is float-trolling from a boat, perhaps the most mobile method of all (see diagrams above). Its effectiveness is only limited by the number of pike that you can present a bait to. On the Broads many pike anglers float-troll with livebaits. This is generally a method which picks up the smaller fish, up to about 15 lb (7 kg), although I can think of one or two thirty-pounders (14 kg) that have fallen to it.

If it does not catch the really big fish on Broadland waters such as the Bure, the method makes up for this failure with abundant action. It will often yield a lot of fish, particularly on those bright sunny days when the water is fairly clear. Float-trolling is not difficult, although it helps to be adept at rowing quietly and getting very close to features such as overhanging trees. A sliding float is used and this can be set so that the bait is just off the bottom, or several feet over depth. A few SSG shot help to keep down the bait, which is mounted head-up the trace. I like to use two rods and I set the drag on the multipliers so that a taking pike can pull line off without difficulty. As it does so, the audible clicking provides a warning additional to that of the float either going under or lying flat.

Fishing in a strong wind

On big waters, when a strong wind is blowing, float-trolling can be extremely difficult. It is possible to use an electric trolling motor to advantage in this situation. It can provide thrust while the oars remain in use for fine-tuning your position. Using the motor on its own for float-trolling is not advisable, because the control you get when rowing is better. Also, you tend to be facing away from your floats and the way a bait is reacting can provide clues as to the whereabouts of pike.

When float-trolling in deep water, a standard sliding-float rig can cause the bait to work up through the float and fail to fish at the desired depth. There are a number of remedies. The simplest is a stop-knot and bead, or a moveable stop made from a 2 mm piece of valve rubber stopped with a piece of matchstick, below the float, set so that the float is 'fixed' at the desired depth. This rig is a bit awkward to get over the side of the boat, especially if you are fishing in 20 ft (6 m) of water. Also, when landing a fish, you have to push the stop-knot down by winding against the float. Des Taylor came up with a novel solution to the problem while fishing at Ardingly. He attached a Gardner clip to his float and then clipped the line into it. There is still the problem of dropping a lot of line over the side, but when you pull into a fish the line pulls out of the clip, leaving the float to slide down freely.

Bob Jackson displays a 20 lb (9 kg) pike taken on a freelined dead roach – a very challenging technique – from a Fenland river.

The Dutch anglers seem to have found the best solution: a self-locking device. This is simply a piece of stiff tube bent into a half moon. The float is attached to the tube and the line goes through the tube. In this way, when the line is under any tension, it locks into position. A similar result can be obtained using a small piece of cane on to which have been whipped two hook eyes set at right angles. The line is threaded through the hook eyes and this arrangement holds the line when it is under tension.

Trolling under power

On bigger waters such as those in Ireland, trolling of deadbaits and lures is usually carried out while under power. In the USA all sorts of aids are used to help the angler troll efficiently. In Britain, however, few of these have caught on. For example, there are cavitation plates which fit on to the back of a large outboard motor, allowing the speed to be reduced when under power. There is a device called a Definder which counts how much line you have out, and there are bite indicators and even trolling-speed indicators. It is possible to do without such aids, but they nevertheless have undoubted benefits.

In its simplest form, trolling while under power is a matter of casting out a couple of baits and dragging them around behind the boat until something attaches itself. Pike can certainly be caught in this way, but a lot more will come aboard if you think about your approach. An echo-sounder is a great help and, if you are using two rods, it is possible to fish at different depths, increasing your chances of picking up pike. When trolling, you work your way around a water, exploring as you go. The echo-sounder shows up the features, which you can make a note of. If a fish turns up in a particular area, so much the better. It takes a surprisingly short time to get to know your way around even a big water. The only problem is that the fish frequently move around and are not always in the same areas.

Generally, you will be trolling baits at 10–15 ft (3–4 m), unless you are using specialized methods such as downriggers or lead-cored line. With baits set at these depths it will be possible to cover depths down to 30 ft (9 m), the pike being drawn up to the baits as the latter pass by. In most cases it is not essential to get a bait down near the bottom. In this way you avoid constant snagging and the accumulation of weed and debris on the hooks.

The author in his younger days shows off two lean fish which he caught on deadbait from a Fenland drain.

A trolled deadbait will usually be either a herring or a trout and have two or three trebles along its flank. Extra lead above the trace will help keep it at the desired depth. Diving plugs will find their own depth as will reasonably heavy spoons. If you are on your own and fishing two rods it is helpful to have one rod on a trolling rest. This is a boat fishing rod rest, which holds the rod yet enables the angler to get to grips with a pike once a take happens.

Downriggers

To get baits fishing at a precise depth, downriggers are used. It is generally thought that a downrigger is used for deep fishing, but this is not the case. Downriggers normally consist of a wire cable on to which is attached a heavy weight of around 6 lb (3 kg). A quick-release clip attached to the weight holds the line and so keeps the lure at the desired depth. The lure or bait is not fished too far behind the weight – say, 10 yards (9 m). With the rod in a holder and bent over because it is under tension from the weight, a take is indicated by the rod springing straight.

The more expensive downriggers have a depth recorder on the cable spool, giving you a precise read-out of the depth. The downrigger is probably the only way to get baits down to depths in excess of 30 ft (9 m), although in the British Isles there is not much evidence that you have to go so deep to catch fish. A lead-cored line will also take a bait down deeper, but if you have to fish deep the downrigger is really the best option.

Before I leave the subject of trolling, I should mention a version of this method that relies on a controlled drift rather than moving under power or oars. There are situations where it is beneficial to cover the water very slowly. Particularly when lure fishing, this may not be possible while under power. The answer is to drift and cast, and retrieve as you do so. Unless the water is fairly calm, the wind will tend to push the boat along a little too fast. The solution is to use a drogue to slow the movement of the boat.

A drogue is an aquatic version of a parachute: it allows water to pass through very slowly and in so doing slows the rate of movement right down. Using the drogue, it is possible to cover the same area several times with a lure before you slowly move into a new area. The drogue is best set from the middle of the boat, and the middle seat or a rowlock is usually a good position for this. If there is a strong swell it is safer to set it from the bows. There are other ways to obtain the same result, but they are rather crude. For example, a light weight dragging the bottom will slow the boat down, but this is inviting a hooked fish to find it and get tangled up.

You can either make a drogue or buy one of the excellent models sold by Bob Church for trout anglers. To make one you simply need a stout circle of canvas with a hole in the middle. Four cords from the canvas to the central ring complete the home-made drogue. In an emergency, if you have not got a drogue, an ET weighing sling will do something to slow the boat, as will a bucket on a rope.

BAITS

Once you have weighed up the basic pike-fishing techniques, you must then consider what type of bait you will use. As with any other aspect of fishing, preferences vary. For livebaiting I have long favoured crucian carp. Their main advantages are that they do not tangle, they work away for hours on end, and they are virtually indestructible. Their only drawback is that they do tend to slow right down when the water temperature is low. Another advantage of crucians is the ease with which they can be trapped using a simple baited fish trap. Few other species will make greater efforts to get into a fish trap. Small common and mirror carp, although not quite as easy to trap, are a good second-best.

The commonest species of all, the roach, is probably the most often used livebait. These, along with chub, dace and bream, work hard, even in cold water. Perch were another favourite of mine, although these days it is pretty rare to come across bait-sized examples. Like crucians, perch try to swim down rather than up and therefore cause few problems with tangles.

Choosing deadbaits

The choice of deadbaits is much wider than it used to be, with a vast selection now available. Once it was a simple choice: a herring or a sprat. Then mackerel came on to the scene. Add to these dead coarse fish, and generally you had a range varied enough to catch pike on most waters. For some reason no one can explain, the smelt

Fresh herring prepared for freezing. Herring are a long-established pike bait, but face stiff competition from mackerel and smelt.

seems to be a better-than-average bait on most waters. It may be that dead smelts are quite natural on many rivers, since these fish expire after spawning in freshwater. However, this does not explain why still-water pike like them so much. Like many other anglers, I use smelt when I can get them, but I am loath to be held to ransom by the price sometimes asked for them.

Sardines are easily obtained and, although rather soft, make a particularly attractive bait, owing to their strong smell. You can sometimes get really big ones (pilchards) and these almost look good enough to eat! Eel chunks have become a very useful bait on some waters, but it is worth noting here that it is rather antisocial to use large eels for bait. Many anglers do not like eels, but, speaking as an eel angler of several years' experience, I would be most unhappy to see fish over a pound (0.5 kg) chopped up for bait. Sandeels are another new bait that have worked for some anglers. Scad, red mullet, capelin, whiting, gurnard – all have been used from time to time. However, I find that pike respond quite well enough to the more usual baits. Trout make good deadbaits since they are quite oily. In coloured water on the Ouse I always used to do well with them once I had cut them in half.

It is not so much what you use for bait as where and when you use it. Take, for example, the humble sprat. A lot of pike are caught each year on this bait simply because there are a lot of sprats being dunked in front of a lot of pike. Sooner or later another thirty-pounder (14 kg) falls to the chap with a sprat under a bung. It is possibly true that the serious pike angler would have caught the same fish on a smelt. But generally the problem is still the same: getting any bait into the right place on the right day.

Bait additives

Some anglers not only get carried away with exotic baits, they also get hooked on flavours and colours. While adding colour to a deadbait in no way detracts from its performance, it is hard to find evidence that coloured deadbaits are superior to ordinary ones. I have used coloured baits and caught pike on them. However, I have not continued to explore this area, simply because, in my view, it is a side issue. The same applies to flavours. Smelt or grayling flavour can do no harm, but neither will it make the pike jump on your baited hooks!

In the end all the technical know-how or equipment can only *help* you catch pike. They cannot on their own do the job. You still have to be up before dawn, get to the swim and cast out. You have to try hard and sometimes have a little luck!

The right choice of bait for the water very much depends on where you are fishing. In practice, each angler has to learn the ropes on his own venues and decide on the right baits to use there. However, some loose guidelines will help the less experienced get started. For example, waters which are seldom fished for pike frequently respond well to lures. Nowhere is this more noticeable than on our trout reservoirs. Here, most of the pike are removed, so they get very little chance to learn from their mistakes. On some days, such has been the success of lures that you would think that there was no other method worth trying.

Unfortunately, on most trout reservoirs livebaiting is not allowed. If it was, then I am sure lure fishing would be less dominant.

107

Whatever you use on a trout reservoir it has to move. While some pike will always end up getting caught on deadbaits, on some waters you could die waiting. Also, it tends to follow that on the smaller trout waters where food fish may vastly outnumber the pike, it is difficult to tempt the few pike present on anything other than a good-sized livebait.

Waters which fail to respond to the static deadbait are rare. Even so, many good anglers have found that waters such as the Severn are not good for static deadbaiting. Wobbled deadbaits will take a lot of fish, but for some reason a bait hard on the bottom attracts little response. Livebaits are generally the best method and on these waters it may pay to fish livebaits on all rods.

Seasonal variations

To add to the pike angler's problems, some waters respond differently from year to year, or even over a season. It is certainly true that some of the Broadland waters vary in their response to dead- and livebaits. The Bure is generally a good deadbait water, yet there

Wobbling a deadbait on a semi-frozen river. Equipped with both deadbait and livebait, you can counter the unpredictability of many waters.

108

are times, particularly early in the season, when a trolled or trotted livebait works infinitely better than a static deadbait. Similarly, on Loch Lomond there are years when deadbaits are very effective and others when nothing but livebaits will work.

Most Fenland drains and gravel pits respond well to deadbaits, particularly old favourites such as smelt. However, it is a foolish angler who relies on just the one method. It is essential to fish both live- and deadbaits on most waters, because sometimes the pike's response tilts marginally and it becomes an 'either or' situation. As a rule, the better the food supply in a water, the longer it takes for a pike to make up its mind. When you realize that the pike in some waters are never particularly hungry, it becomes clear that you must either sit and wait or use my tactics: keep moving in the hope of finding a pike that does want a meal.

Waters where the pike have to work hard to find their food will generally produce a very quick response. On some lochs you can safely assume that if you put a bait near a pike there is a very good chance of a swift take. Mobile tactics are used in such situations to

A 24 lb (11 kg) pike taken on roach livebait from Vernatt's Drain, near Spalding, Lincolnshire, in 1976 — at that time the author's best fish.

109

try and find pike, since fishing only in one spot on a water several miles long is not going to be productive if the nearest pike is half a mile (1 km) away!

Productive areas

Another point well worth remembering is that pike are seldom solitary. Frequently, where there is one big pike there will be another. It is therefore worth concentrating on one swim once a good-sized fish has been caught. As you learn to fish a water you will get to know the areas which consistently produce big pike. You may also learn where the pike are at certain times of the year. On the Ormesby group of broads, the pike feed extensively on fry at certain times of the year. If you have fished the water a lot, it will be clear where to go each time.

On the Thurne and Bure systems there is a huge area of broad connected to the river itself. On the Thurne the pike spend much of the year on the broads out of the way of the boat traffic. Although fish do venture out on to the river, they generally only move because of either angling pressure or a prolonged cold spell. The roach and bream in the Thurne also move around a lot and areas such as Potter Heigham can be alive with these fish in the winter. Sometimes the pike move in on them, but in these days of great angling pressure they do not stay around long. If the weather is exceptionally mild, then the chances are that the pike stay put. And as most of the Thurne broads are inaccessible for most of the winter, that is that!

On the Bure, pike can be found on both the broads and the river all the year round. However, in the depths of winter a lot of food fish end up in the boat basins and the pike are quick to follow. The big pike of the Bure are a mystery. Do they live on the river and simply seldom get caught, or are they tucked away on some private broad, from which they swim out and are unlucky enough to get caught? I doubt if anyone knows the answer.

GETTING TO KNOW A WATER

While it is easy for the experienced pike angler to go to a water and pick a good area to start in, this is not the case for the newcomer to the sport. The most difficult part of pike fishing is getting started. It

An 18¾ lb (8.5 kg) summer-caught fish taken from a shallow bay on a livebait fished right up against water-lily pads.

is no good looking at the angling magazines and thinking that you will soon be catching pike like those you see displayed there. What you do not see in their pages is the majority of anglers who fail to catch big pike.

Whenever you start pike fishing on a new water it is essential to mentally note every detail that you come across. Only by doing this will you put enough information together to enable you to catch fish there consistently. On a gravel pit, for example, by fishing widely you may well find a very specific feature in one swim, a feature unique to that swim and the only one like it on the whole water. You could find the feature by pre-session exploration or you could stumble on it while fishing. It could be a gravel bar or a channel. On the day you fish, the feature might not produce any pike, but it is bound to be worth noting and it may well be attractive to pike. You should also make a note of any spot where you see another angler catch a fish. At a later date the swim will be worth a try.

In your early days of pike fishing it pays to concentrate your efforts on one particular water and get to know it. By all means listen to what information you can pick up from other anglers, but try to keep an open mind, especially when, for example, you come across the local expert who says that all the pike are caught by fishing close to the reeds. The truth may be that he never tries any other areas! I remember being told that one particular water I fished was a 'herring' water. This was quite interesting because I then proceeded to catch some very large pike to over 30 lb (14 kg) on livebaits.

Significant features

Fen drains in particular can come as a bit of a shock to the angler who has never had to tackle a very long water. Various writers have referred to the obvious features such as where side drains enter. However, what do you do when such features do not exist? What you do is look closely at where you are fishing and decide what feature is there that makes that section of drain slightly different. It might only be a slight increase in depth or a few scattered reedbeds. However on featureless waters, anything like this can count for a lot.

There is also the possibility in some drains and rivers that the pike will prefer one bank to the other. The angler who does not explore his swim fully by fishing all the way across may well miss out on a lot

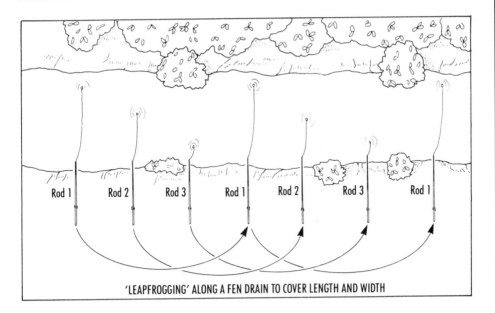

'LEAPFROGGING' ALONG A FEN DRAIN TO COVER LENGTH AND WIDTH

of sport. It is quite possible to fish the wrong side of a wide river and catch nothing. Meanwhile, someone else can turn up and fish the other side and have a great day. It is far better to position your baits so as to cover the full width of the water being fished. When fishing with others, you could try the method shown above.

On some waters long-distance casting may be the only answer to reaching the pike (see diagram on page 114). This generally entails the use of a 3 lb (1.35 kg) test, 12 ft (365 cm) rod and either a good distance-casting bait such as half a mackerel or a small deadbait and a 3 oz (85 g) lead. All this is standard equipment for many big-water anglers. For really long-distance work there are now available coned-spool reels by Daiwa and Shimano. Couple these with shock leaders and it should be possible to get baits beyond the 100-yard (90 m) mark in favourable conditions.

Handling pike

Much of what I have mentioned is specialized fishing and not every-one will have to resort to these tactics. However, if you intend to catch big fish it may be necessary to brush up on your pike handling. These days a lot of carp anglers are switching to pike when the going gets hard. This may be a case of swopping a 'boilie' for a smelt and

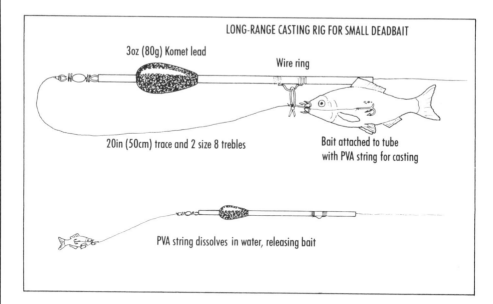

LONG-RANGE CASTING RIG FOR SMALL DEADBAIT

3oz (80g) Komet lead

Wire ring

20in (50cm) trace and 2 size 8 trebles

Bait attached to tube with PVA string for casting

PVA string dissolves in water, releasing bait

then sitting there for three days. But you will get no marks at all if once you have landed the pike you have no idea of what to do with it. Pike are not like carp: they have a set of sharp teeth and it is surprising how many anglers still prod at the fish hopefully without really knowing how to handle the fish so as not to cause harm either to it or themselves.

Precautions against harming the fish

The first step is to put the landed fish somewhere it cannot damage itself. On the bank this will mean on grass, while in a boat you have no choice but to carry something soft to lay the pike on. If you try and handle a pike on a bank that is rough, then the fish will lose scales and suffer abrasions. It may also bang its head while struggling. It also helps if the surface you are working on is wet. In this way less of the pike's protective slime will be removed.

The pike is more afraid of you than vice versa. But remember that its mouth is full of sharp teeth, although it has no intention of using them on you. If you are careless you will get cut, but you are unlikely to be bitten. A pike cannot reason and is not waiting for you to stick your hands in its mouth. However, if you are stupid enough to do so, then you are asking for trouble. Besides, there is no need.

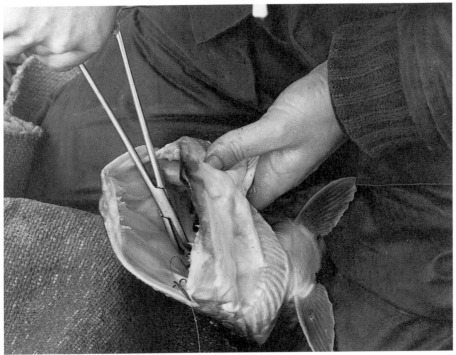

Unhooking a pike. The teeth are a reminder of the importance of positioning the left hand so as to hold the jaws open safely.

UNHOOKING

First, you must control the fish by gently holding it down or sitting astride it holding its head. Do not try to do anything at all until the fish has ceased to thrash about. Then, using your left hand if you are right-handed, or vice versa, slip your finger under the chin. It helps if you wear a good strong glove. You can buy a variety of industrial or gardening gloves suitable for this, or a special unhooking glove. These all protect the fingers from the rows of small teeth on the gill rakers. It is best to use them if you are inexperienced.

With your finger under the jaw and the pike laid on its back, it is a simple job to peer inside the fish's mouth and locate the hooks. If you struck straight away as you should have done, the hooks should be in the side of the mouth, in the roof or sometimes around the tongue. Using a pair of forceps, it is easy enough to remove the hooks without getting your working hand anywhere near the teeth. If the pike does not like this, then remove your finger and hold the fish steady until it ceases to move. Then try again.

No one is perfect and sometimes a set of hooks will end up in the fish's throat. Once again, get the pike upside down and sit astride it with your finger under the chin. If you have a friend with you it will help if he holds the trace for you. He should keep a little tension on the trace so that you can work your forceps through the posterior set of gill rakers. With tension on the trace, it should be possible to see the first treble, provided the bait is no longer on the hooks. If it is, you will have to move the bait out of the way.

Sometimes, if you are really lucky, the bait comes out with the hooks in it. If it does not, then grasp the tail of the bait with the forceps and pull it out. Once the bait is clear, the first treble can be grasped through the gills with the forceps. The advantage of artery forceps is that they can be clamped on the hooks, leaving you free to turn the hooks upside down. If you have difficulty clearing the flesh from the hooks, turn them back the other way. With a bit of jiggling the hooks will usually come clear. The same procedure is followed with the second treble. If you are careful semi-barbless hooks can be removed wherever they are without any damage to the pike. Whatever you do, avoid brute force. Tearing the gut wall can allow digestive juices to enter the body cavity with potentially fatal results. While forceps can be very efficient at removing hooks, there are a number of products such as the Deep Throat disgorger which are helpful to the novice pike angler. It does no harm to try these pieces of equipment, although most experienced pike anglers can cope quite well with the humble forceps.

A responsible approach

There should be no need to leave hooks in pike, although from time to time you read in the angling press of a fish so badly hooked that the line was cut and the pike released with the hooks still in. If you are an absolute novice and this happens it is perhaps to be expected. However, lack of adequate unhooking equipment is in no way excusable. If you are going to fish for pike, you must make sure that you are properly equipped to return the fish alive and well.

If you are fishing alone and are inexperienced, hook removal can

David 'Pondo' Pond is understandably pleased with a 22 lb (10 kg) fish he took on deadbait from Martham Broad on Norfolk's River Thurne.

be more difficult, but never be afraid to ask for help if you have problems. Most of us deal with deep hooks single handed by grasping the line between our teeth and using this instead of a friend's hand. In either case, remain alert to the movements of the pike, especially when your hand is only a few inches from its snout.

Once safely unhooked, the fish will be weighed if it is of a worthwhile size or slipped straight back. A good-sized weigh sling such as the ET model is ideal for carrying the fish back to the water. Before weighing the fish, the sling should first be wetted and the excess water shaken off. Then the scales are zeroed before the pike is placed in the sling. If you want a photograph, it is best to control the fish by holding it under its chin. If it struggles, hold it to your body and do not let it fall to the ground. Never stand up with the fish for a picture, since the nearer it is to the ground the less the likelihood of a bad fall.

When taking photographs it is essential to get everything organized beforehand. With the pike safely retained in the landing net, a sack or a tube, it is a simple job to get everything ready before you actually hold the fish. A fish should not be out of water for longer than three minutes. In fact, most photo sessions need last only a minute. The big problem today is that the average angler has several cameras and a video as well. The result is that pike are spending much longer on the bank than they ought to. This may be all right in winter when a pike's metabolism is low and the fight it puts up is relatively poor. But in summer and autumn, it is very dangerous to delay the fish's return. When you see videos of pike that keel over when they are put back, then you know that something is amiss.

The retention of pike for group pictures is another debatable subject. One pike on the bank is a lot of hard work, two can be difficult, and any more than that can be a real handful. The simple answer is not to retain pike for multiple-fish shots. We have all done it in the past, but nowadays most pike anglers catch a fish and return it straightaway. But if you are getting frequent runs or the light is poor, then by all means put a fish in a sack until the time is right for a photograph. In any case, once in a while another big fish follows the first one and then you have two good pike to photograph.

With more and more pressure on pike these days and some fish getting caught four or fives times a season, the pike angler must take greater care than ever to handle his catch correctly. If only 10 per cent of us accidentally kill the fish we catch, it will have the same effect as that produced by the smaller number of pike anglers who killed their fish in the bad old days.

If you are new to the sport, then join the Pike Anglers' Club (PAC) and ask the right questions at talks and teach-ins. There will always be someone who will help you out. At the time of writing membership costs £10 per annum. Write to: Pete Haywood, 20 Carisbrooke Avenue, Gedling, Nottingham NG4 2RD

CHAPTER SIX

MEMORIES OF BIG PIKE

Pike fishing has a long history, but the farther back you go the less reliable tends to be the information and sometimes fact tends to merge with fiction. For the majority of modern anglers the most impressive big fish are those caught in our own lifetime. So without doubt the first of the fish which deserves a mention is Peter Hancock's 40 lb (18 kg) pike, caught from Horsey Mere in Norfolk in 1967.

Horsey Mere had long enjoyed a reputation for big pike, even though in 1938 the sea had broken through the defences and killed everything in the water. Luckily Edwin Vincent spent a lot of time and effort restocking the water. By the early 1960s the Mere was fast becoming a Mecca for pike anglers from all over Britain. Many anglers who have since become well known caught their first big pike from this water. Local anglers such as Dennis Pye, Frank Wright, Bill Giles and Reg Sandys were also fishing it hard and a lot of big fish of over 20 lb (9 kg) and even over 30 lb (14 kg) were caught there. At the time several people were convinced that Horsey would produce a forty-pounder (18 kg), but little did the modest Peter Hancock realize that fate was to deal him a very kind hand.

A boat-fishing water

Horsey Mere is about 100 acres (45 hectares), reed-lined, and has very little bank fishing. Therefore most anglers fish it from a boat. It is nowhere very deep, with 7 ft (2 m) the maximum depth. The Mere can be extremely weedy in places and the water colour varies from crystal clear to bright orange. The latter colour is due to the iron-laden water that is pumped into the Mere from the low-level drainage system. The water is also very saline and this can lead to the bloom or a certain algae known as *Prymnesium parva*. This algae

RECENT BIG PIKE

44 lb 14 oz (20.5 kg)	M. Linton	1987	Ardleigh Reservoir, Essex
44 lb 8 oz (20 kg)*	C. Garratt	1988	Llandegfedd Reservoir, Wales
44 lb (20 kg)**	S. Gilham	1988	Llandegfedd Reservoir, Wales
43 lb 2 oz (19.5 kg)	P. Wright	1988	Castle Howard Lake, Yorkshire
43 lb 2 oz (19.5 kg)**	B. Ingrams	1988	Llandegfedd Reservoir, Wales
42 lb 5 oz (19 kg)*	P. Climo	1988	Llandegfedd Reservoir, Wales
42 lb 2 oz (19 kg)†	D. Amies	1985	River Thurne, Norfolk
41 lb 6 oz (18.5 kg)†	N. Fickling	1985	River Thurne, Norfolk
41 lb 4 oz (18.5 kg)†	J. Mills	1986	River Thurne, Norfolk
40 lb (18 kg)	P. Hancock	1967	Horsey Mere, Norfolk
39 lb 8 oz (18 kg)	D. Leary	1983	Lyng Trout Fishery, Norfolk
39 lb (17.5 kg)	C. Loveland	1967	Knipton Reservoir, Leicestershire
39 lb (17.5 kg)	L. Tyler	1985	Broadlands Lake, Hampshire
38 lb 4 oz (17.5 kg)	P. Emmings	1969	Abberton Reservoir, Essex
38 lb 1 oz (17 kg)	J. Watson	1988	Thurne system, Norfolk
38 lb (17 kg)†	S. Lampard	1985	River Thurne, Norfolk

Note: SI (metric) weights are given to the nearest half kilogram.
*, **, and † denote the same fish in each case.

releases a toxin when it dies which is lethal to fish. There is little doubt that the algae had been present for a number of years. Fortunately, it had never had a serious effect on the pike population.

On 2 February 1967, such problems were the last thing on Peter Hancock's mind. Peter was a local farmer and had plenty to keep him busy throughout the year. However, he did like to get away when he could to fish on his own for pike. With such sessions in mind, he had acquired a converted ship's lifeboat, which could be used as a home during his occasional fishing trips. Although he had fished Horsey for a number of years, it had not been particularly kind to him. Yet on that memorable day, Horsey was nevertheless where he headed. The weather conditions were ideal with a water temperature of 5° C (42 F) and an air temperature of 10° C (50° F). There is nothing more certain to get the pike feeding than a rise in temperature after a cold spell and the pike in waters such as Horsey seem to respond particularly well to such fluctuations.

Like so many other anglers before and after him, Peter's starting-point for the fishing trip was Martham Ferry. A small and ancient outboard motor meant that the journey took a good hour, yet it is

Martyn Page with a 28 lb 15 oz (13 kg) pike and Steve Harper with a 22 lb 6 oz (10 kg) fish, both taken on roach livebait on the Broads.

always a pleasant trip, wending your way up Candle Dyke and then entering the reed-lined expanses of Heigham Sound. Then there is a right turn up Meadow Dyke and the long narrow channel that leads suddenly, when you least expect it, into Horsey Mere itself. Facing you as you enter, slightly to the left is the boathouse and the reed island. To the right is Horsey Mill, the only feature to significantly break the monotony of the flat horizon.

Heavy duty tackle

The wind was a fresh south-westerly, which suggested that the shelter of the west bank would be advisable. It was after all three years since Peter had fished the Mere and there was no point in suffering on this exploratory trip. He was using two rods: one with livebait, the other with ledgered dead roach. Like many other anglers at that time, he had discovered that a ledgered deadbait would tend to produce a fairly high average size of pike. The rods were not quite what we would use today, being 5 ft (150 cm) glass-fibre spinning rods, but with 15 lb (7 kg) line there was no reason why Peter should not land anything that Horsey could produce. His terminal tackle was likewise typical of the period, consisting of a No. 4 snap tackle. He had found a few weed-free places where he could fish a livebait. Meanwhile the dead roach was ledgered, with a small pilot float for bite indication.

Peter settled down to enjoy the atmosphere of the place and indeed few people who fish the water could fail to recognize that it has something special that sets it apart from most others. For one thing, the variety of wildlife present provides hours of diversion from the fishing itself. The water is owned by the National Trust and leased to John Buxton, the son of the previous owner Major Anthony Buxton.

After an hour Peter noticed Edwin Vincent and two companions pass by and head for the south bank. He continued to work along the west bank, trying each new swim until eventually he reached the mouth of Waxham Cut. At this point it is a little deeper and less weedy. The water is also very coloured because this is where the iron-polluted water is pumped in. Peter had not long cast out when there was a slight movement of the pilot float. He wound in the livebait and then tightened up to the deadbait, even though there had been no further movement. When he contacted the fish, he realized it was a good one and played it gently because the day before he had lost a small fish when his 15 lb (7 kg) line snapped. The fish bored deeply in short runs, trying to wrap itself around the anchor rope. After twenty minutes he was convinced that it was a twenty-pounder (9 kg), but had no idea that he would be doubling this figure when the fish was finally landed and weighed.

The moment of truth

As happens to many anglers playing a big fish for a long time, Peter's attention wandered and he found himself trying to decipher the words on a sign some distance away. After twenty-five minutes the pike came up on the surface and although it was clear that it was a big fish, without getting a good look at its depth it was impossible to tell just how big. The moment of truth was drawing near, for in those days large landing nets were not generally in use. Therefore the fish had to be gaffed. Just imagine the strength required to lift such a huge fish over the side of a boat, with a hook under its jaw. It would be difficult to bring a fish this big into a boat in a landing net!

Luckily, the huge pike had put up all the resistance it was going to, allowing itself to be gaffed cleanly and lifted into the boat. Once it was aboard, Peter covered the pike with a sack and paused to wonder at its sheer size. There had been some big pike caught from Horsey in recent years, but nothing within even 6 lb (2.7 kg) of this monster. He then raised anchor and headed for Edwin Vincent's boat. Edwin and his companions were dumbstruck on sight of the fish, something few had really expected to see from a Broadland water. They went to the island and weighed the fish on two sets of scales and a weight of 40 lb (18 kg) was recorded. The fish was 47½ in (122 cm) long, with a girth of 26 in (66 cm). In the true sporting tradition the fish was returned after a number of photographs had been taken.

The fish was, as far as we know, never caught again, but in reality there was little chance of this because in August 1969 the worst outbreak of *Prymnesium* flared up, leaving Horsey Mere desolated. Some of the regulars on the water were in tears as countless big pike floated up to the surface. If Hancock's pike was remarkable, so was the disaster that followed. Though Horsey did make something of a recovery in the 1980s, it has never reached the peak of the late 1960s. Each year fish continue to die and the fishing there is very hard. Yet there is always the chance of another huge fish, the likes of which made for a very memorable 'Hancock's Half Hour'.

The big pike return

While Horsey died, the other end of the Thurne system had not suffered quite as badly. Unsuspected by most anglers, the pike re-established themselves around Martham Broad and by 1982 the big fish were back. Naturally, as the next couple of years passed by, a lot of anglers started to show an interest in these fish. Many anglers caught their first thirty-pounder (14 kg) from Martham Broad, but soon the poaching was to end. The problem was that the local Naturalists' Trust laid claim to the two broads and did not allow fishing. Eventually, the North Broad was opened on a limited basis, but the South Broad remained firmly closed. It was frustrating for all those fishing the area, because the South Broad was for some reason the water that produced the really big fish of over 35 lb (16 kg). However, for the time being the big pike remained undisturbed.

Several anglers had noticed that at certain times of the year and in certain conditions big pike appeared on the River Thurne itself. The fishing pattern then started to change, with more anglers concentrating their efforts on the river rather than on the broads. Neville Fickling was one such angler. He had, like many others, caught some good fish from the broads, yet had had little success on the river. However, as the fishing tailed off on the North Broad he devoted more of his attention to the Thurne itself, particularly between Dungeon's Corner and Martham Ferry. Neville had made slow progress up to December 1985, but just before the weather began to deteriorate he managed to catch a fish of just over 20 lb (9 kg) from a spot near the Ferry.

There then followed a very cold spell, the likes of which few of us could remember. It snowed and everywhere froze over. It was not until the end of January that the mild weather returned. Every water in the country was probably fished to its limits that week, but Neville disregarded everywhere else and headed for the Thurne. The first day near the Ferry was uneventful, so the next day he moved farther upriver. Just as seems to have happened to many of the anglers in the past who have caught big pike, fate took a hand. Neville decided to fish a swim he had tried once before with no result. The first run of the morning came on a smelt and when he struck he was convinced, just like Peter Hancock, that it was a big fish. Yet during the brief fight it never seemed likely that the fish would be particularly large. However, on netting the pike, it became obvious that this was something out of the ordinary.

A new record

Once it had been weighed, photographed and released, it was clear that this fish had soundly beaten the old record. At 41 lb 6 oz (19 kg) it was the biggest pike for many years. Neville added a nineteen-pounder (9 kg) and a sixteen-pounder (7 kg) on the same day, followed by a fish of 32 lb 8 oz (15 kg) the next day. All in all, a memorable three days. What had probably happened was that the cold weather had driven the pike out of the South Broad into the river. Such events do not happen every year and someone was destined to catch that fish while it was on the river. Neville was the lucky angler, but luck can only play its part if you are there making the effort. Later, it became clear that the pike was a known fish that Neville himself had caught about eighteen months earlier from the same broad.

The story does not end there, however, because the fish was to make several more appearances the following season. As fate would have it, *Prymnesium* struck again in 1986 and it was another major outbreak. Horsey was seriously affected and up at Martham Broad the pike were forced to move out into the river. The local anglers were quick to realize that there were a large number of big pike on the river and soon a lot of fishing effort was being directed at these unfortunate fish. Derek Amies caught the big fish again, this time weighing 42 lb 2 oz (19 kg) and later in the season the same fish came out twice more, but was never seen again.

An exceptional season

My own most memorable capture does not stand alone in my memory but as part of an unforgettable season when almost everything seemed to go right for me. But then I worked hard for all the fish I caught and took some risks. At the end of 1986 I had spent too much time fishing and ended up taking a break until the following summer. Then my good friends Bob Jackson and David Pond coaxed me back to the waterside. The summer was spent enjoying lighthearted fishing. We caught plenty of fish, although nothing particularly big.

As autumn approached I started to put in some before-work sessions on the River Bure at Horning. The first of these yielded fish of 16 lb 8 oz (7.5 kg) and 14 lb (6.5 kg). This was not bad for a quick visit, so I felt I had to return the following day for a longer session. When the fish are coming out, it is surprising how easy it is to get out of bed well before dawn. The next couple of mornings yielded a few more fish over 10 lb (4.5 kg) and I kept the pressure on, this time with a brief bank-fishing session.

I had a big roach deadbait I had scooped out of the water the previous day. I do not usually use such large baits, but if one does turn up for free I am loath to throw it away. Needless to say, when the bobbin dropped off it was on the rod with the big roach. The fish

The author in the middle of a tussle with a good-sized pike on a Norfolk river in winter.

felt heavy and put up little resistance. It did not look like a well fish and my doubts began after I tried to return it. It would not swim off. To cut a long and sad story short, the fish eventually died. She weighed 25 lb 3 oz (11.5 kg) and I was somewhat thrown for a few weeks while I got over the loss.

Unfortunately, the river started to get really busy, so it was time to move on to another water. I pottered about on a local river, exploring new areas and catching fish to 18 lb 2 oz (8 kg) as I did so. However, the river's potential for big fish was taking a long time to be realized, and between visits I spent some time fishing a very private broad. The results were not brilliant and for a while I fished here and there, not managing to get set into a really productive pattern. I also tried a few trips to Ormesby Broad, taking along a couple of friends. They did quite well, with fish to 22 lb 8 oz (10 kg), while I had three to 17 lb 12 oz (8 kg). Everyone left in a good mood!

A good day for poaching

By the time Christmas Day had come around, Bob Jackson was itching to try somewhere special. It was a water that was almost impossible to fish, unless of course you picked a day when most self-respecting anglers and wardens were at home. Although I had fished this particular broad, Bob had not, and as everyone else had fished it in the past, it seemed a good idea to give it a try. The whole exercise had to be carried out with commando-like stealth, our inspiration being the motto 'He who does not get discovered lives to fish another day'! We launched the boat very quietly well before dawn and rowed up the river to the broad.

We arrived at first light and for a while struggled to find the secret entrance. After a lot of pushing, shoving and rowing we eventually emerged on to the broad, probably the first anglers to do so in a long time. The fact that it was a misty day encouraged us because it would help to avoid detection. We arrived at a spot which used to produce fish in the past and put out a couple of free-swimming livebaits. Bob had a nine-pounder (4 kg) straightaway, followed by a two-pounder (0.9 kg) as he wound his bait in. These were not quite the giant fish we had expected, but they were pike and at least we were getting some action.

We moved, but now the mist was beginning to clear. Some people walked by on the bank, yet they never noticed us. It is strange, but it seems easier to detect movement on the bank from a boat than vice versa. The move did one thing for us: it showed quite clearly where the pike were because we spooked a couple of big fish. Reasoning that this was as good a place as any to stop, we dropped anchor and put the rods out again. On his first cast Bob had a seven-pounder (3 kg) and a few minutes later he happened to be standing up when he noticed a big pike swim by the end of the boat. This in itself is unusual on any water, but my reaction was almost automatic and I quickly dropped a livebait in near to where the pike had passed by. However, after a while there had been no response so I went back to fishing my own patch of water.

Just after Bob had recast, his float slid away and he bent into what seemed a modest fish. But, as is often the case, the fish became heavier as the fight went on. This probably happens because the fish tends to take a while to realize that it is hooked and puts up a big struggle only when it is clear that something is amiss. The first time the pike approached the net it was clear that it was not having anything to do with it. In the water it looked like a big fish, but unless you see the depth of the fish it is not easy to determine its size. One thing was for certain: it had the head of a typical Thurne pike, like a crocodile! Once we had it in the boat it was clear that it was not as fat as it could have been. Still, it weighed a very nice 27 lb 8 oz (12.5 kg), a personal best for Bob after putting in a lot of effort with pike. We stayed and fished all day although the weather turned bright, sunny and calm: hardly conducive to good pike fishing. Despite the weather, Bob had a run on a deadbait which on striking felt like the proverbial brick wall. Unfortunately, the pike came off. On this water you can never tell what is going to happen next.

Holiday sport

Over the Christmas period, the fishing went quite well and with the extra holiday time I fished as hard as possible, spending time on all the likely venues in the area. Another private broad we call Donkey Broad had not seen much attention from us in recent weeks, so we decided to give it a try. Getting boats overland does not become any easier the older you get! The last time we had visited the water, there had been some shooters on the bank and we had decided there and then that we would leave it for a while. Donkey Broad is very shallow, only 3 ft (1 m) deep, and can turn pretty clear in winter. So although it is a very good pike water, the fish do not always give themselves up.

We rowed very quietly to our chosen spot and put the baits out. I had the first two fish, small ones on drifted livebaits. Next, Bob started with a fish of 16 lb 4 oz (7.5 kg) on dead roach. I then air-injected my own dead roach and started to twitch it back towards the boat. A gentle pull indicated that something had latched on to the bait. This proved to be a nice fish of 17 lb 10 oz (8 kg). Finally, another small fish heralded the end of sport in that part of the broad. We moved to an area that Bob fancied, yet which I had never fished before. From noon until 1 pm I had a very hectic time, with good-sized pike trying to climb up my rods! There were in all five fish over 10 lb (4.5 kg) to add to the others I had caught, the best weighing 18 lb 8 oz (8.5 kg). This gave me a total of 125 lb (57 kg) – first-class pike fishing by anyone's reckoning. One fish even took a smelt dangling over the side of the boat after I had wound in and put that rod out of the way.

A trip to Donkey Broad

A few days were spent on the Bure at Wroxham and other local waters. It is always a good idea to keep your ear to the ground in an area such as Norfolk, because you can then find out whether various waters are fishing well or not. The Bure in particular is very changeable, with one trip when the pike are 'on' worth half a dozen of the other kind. Eventually the urge to fish Donkey Broad became irresistible and this time David Pond joined me. As luck would have it, he gave me a sound thrashing. I caught four small ones to his two of 18 lb 4 oz (8.5 kg) and 16 lb 4 oz (7.5 kg). The latter fell for a wobbled mackerel head, which is something of a weird method to use! We returned the next day, but it was flat calm and we dared not move around much in case we alerted someone to our presence. Still, the static approach worked well enough, with three runs to my rod producing three fish of up to 17 lb 10 oz (8 kg).

The next day saw a total change of direction. It seemed a good idea to give Martham North Broad a try. David had never fished the water, so we set off to give him his first taste of Thurne Broad pike fishing. We arrived and headed straight for a narrow channel at the back of the broad. Here we were fairly out of the way, and what is more, the swim was a really good one, an area where I had caught many big fish in the past. It was nice to sit and anticipate what was to come, with the wind whispering in the reeds behind us. However, we hardly had chance to do this because the rod with the herring was bouncing within five minutes. That fish weighed 17 lb 12 oz (8 kg) and was followed in two hours by a fish of 11 lb 14 oz (5.5 kg) and then a thirteen-pounder (6 kg). We then moved into a long bay on the east side of the broad and I promptly caught the same fish of 11 lb 14 oz again. It even took the same bait, a smelt. After then pulling out of a fish on the strike, a dead roach went on to yield a very long twenty-one pounder (9.5 kg).

My young companion was by this time wondering what he had to do to get a run. Fortunately for his sanity, his first fish turned out to be a beauty of 23 lb 12 oz (11 kg). Just to prove that things come in threes he then caught in quick succession fish of 9 lb 12 oz (4.5 kg) and 23 lb 1 oz (10.5 kg). Now the roles had been reversed and it looked as if my rods would be redundant for the rest of the session. Once that swim had gone dead we moved again and this time I started to catch. The run on half a mackerel turned out to be from a fish of 22 lb 5 oz (10 kg) and then the dead roach yielded one of 17 lb 14 oz (8 kg).

After that the rest of the session was uneventful, but a few days later we returned and, starting where we had caught fish the previous trip, it was soon clear that the fish had moved. Over on the west side of the broad, my first fish was 9 lb 4 oz (4 kg), but after that I just sat back and watched. Five good pike came to David's rods, including one of 22 lb 8 oz (10 kg). The next day I caught the same pike, so it looked as if the really big fish were no longer to be found on the broad. The combination of *Prymnesium* and intense angling pressure had finally taken its toll.

A theory discredited

Just because things were going so well, it was inevitable that the weather had to start to get colder. Despite the air temperature dropping to −4° C (25° F) overnight, David and I went to Donkey Broad. Now in theory a really cold night ought to put the pike well

A River Thurne pike of 30 lb 3 oz (18 kg) caught in high summer on a free-swimming livebait.

and truly off the feed. However, the pike had obviously not heard of the same theories as I had and decided to feed really well. David managed just one small one, while I had my revenge with fish of 20 lb 1 oz (9 kg), 18 lb 4 oz (8.5 kg), 12 lb 4 oz (5.5 kg), and two small ones.

The weather became very wet and cold after this and we failed to catch much on the next few trips. Then, against my better judgement, Bob and I went up to fish Horsey Mere. Now normally you can fish there during the closed period without any problems, provided you keep out of sight. But this time we caught nothing and, to add to our problems, we got caught! So we left somewhat sheepishly and moved back down Meadow Dyke to find somewhere else to fish.

On the way up to Horsey we had set a few markers to try and find some pike. These consisted of herrings tied to cotton. If a pike picked one up, the marker would either move or the cotton would break, allowing the marker to drift away. The idea was to cover a large area of water. On this part of the Thurne system the pike are

Pike of 25 lb 6 oz and 25 lb 2 oz (11.5 kg) caught on a float-ledgered half mackerel on successive casts from Donkey Broad.

few and far between, although past experience has indicated that some very big fish could turn up. When we got back to where we had set the markers one of them had gone. I tried to grab the marker when we eventually found it, but the fish powered off. I then cast over the line, intent on looking at what had grabbed the herring, but the pike ejected it in disgust.

We set some more markers and returned a few days later. This time a few of the markers had gone and we tried several of the spots where fish activity had been noted. We caught nothing and after an hour and a half I wanted to move, but David wanted to stay put. In the end we agreed to have some coffee and then move. By now it was pouring with rain and when I picked the rod up I thought initially that it was snagged on something. Most snags do not kick back, so even I realized that I had something hanging on the end. When we netted her I was really pleased, because at 23 lb (10.5 kg) the fish was a somewhat unexpected bonus.

All this had happened by 9.45 am, and after slipping the fish back I put on a fresh herring, stabbing it well to release plenty of juices. The next twenty minutes were spent little knowing what was about to follow. I was looking away from my float, but David noticed that something was happening. My attention having been drawn to the float, I picked up the rod and wound down, to be met by a solid resistance. The fish promptly headed for the boat, before deciding that this was perhaps not advisable. It felt like a good fish, but I did not get a good look at it until it was in the net.

A weighty problem

We both realized that this was one of the big ones and it took the two of us to lift the net plus fish into the boat. There seemed to be little room for the two of us and this giant fish in our small boat. When we weighed her, the best we could get was 34 lb (15.5 kg), the scales at their limit. We did not have a bigger set of scales with us – after all, you just do not expect to get a fish that large. So we took a couple of quick photographs and I went off to find Bob Jackson and a bigger set of scales.

When I returned with him we weighed the fish properly and the scales settled at 38 lb 1 oz (17 kg) – definitely one of the big ones! The fish was only 46 in (117 cm) long, so she was very thick across the back and deep. She was then returned and I wondered if she would ever be seen again. The next time that pike turned up, who could tell how big she would be! The next weekend we kept away from that area, returning during the following week. After a couple of hours there was a run on the half mackerel. It was another big one, this time 27 lb 10 oz (12.5 kg). A while later I had a repeat capture: the twenty-three pounder of a few days earlier, now weighing 22 lb 8 oz (10 kg).

Several further trips proved to be blanks and that was the end of that particularly productive interlude. This is so often the case on the Thurne. You find a handful of fish, do well and then go back to struggling, no matter how much effort you put in. Such a catch was bound to attract unwanted attention from other pike anglers without the initiative to try new areas, so the following day I headed for Martham and met several anglers. I added a fish of 22 lb 13 oz (10.5 kg) for my efforts. The rest of the season faded out with no more really spectacular catches. Realistically, I could hardly expect much more and I was well satisfied, having at last put my hooks into something really big. The fascination of the whole Broadland area is that it is big enough for one or two pike to grow undisturbed into really big fish. There are so few fish over 35 lb (16 kg) in England that it is comforting to think that some of them are in my own area.

CHAPTER SEVEN

WHERE TO FIND BIG PIKE

I have restricted the scope of this chapter to waters which have the potential to produce pike of over 30 lb (14 kg) in England, Scotland, Wales and Ireland. These are the waters where most British pike anglers spend their time.

Scotland

The obvious first choice in Scotland for big pike must be Loch Lomond. This huge water has over the years produced a number of fish over 35 lb (16 kg), although none has exceeded this weight by a large margin. Loch Lomond is currently facing a lot of angling pressure and some anglers are now equipped with big boats with powerful motors, making all areas of the loch fishable. A thirty-pounder (14 kg) from Lomond is a very big fish and few anglers are likely to catch one this size. Nevertheless, there is always the chance of a freak fish and one day some lucky angler will catch a pike there which will give 40 lb (18 kg) a close nudge.

Not far away is Loch Awe, a water which has improved a lot in recent years. It has produced the odd thirty-pounder (14 kg), probably the result of massive escapes of caged rainbow trout into the loch. It is certainly a water to watch in the near future, although there are a number of fishing restrictions such as a ban on camping, caused by people who have been catching the rainbow trout to sell in Glasgow.

There are other lochs in Scotland worth trying, such as Loch Tay, but many are gill-netted and the pike suffer badly from persecution. There are also a number of put-and-take trout fisheries that we in England hear little of. Loch Ken, a little farther south, has been badly affected by pike killing and as far as most pike anglers are concerned is a waste of time.

Dave Holden shows off a 12½ lb (5.5 kg) pike he coaxed out of a backwater on the River Lune in Lancashire.

England

Many Lancashire anglers are now travelling to the Lake District to fish and although there have been one or two thirty-pounders (14 kg), there is little evidence to suggest that something bigger is going to turn up. Farther east, near York, is Castle Howard Lake, which recently produced a giant of a pike at 43 lb 2 oz (19.5 kg). This was a bit of a surprise, but it goes to show that a large productive water can throw up an enormous fish despite all the predictions of the pundits. Yorkshire, for some reason, has produced some very big pike over the years, most unconfirmed, but several trout waters near Sheffield such as Dam Flask continue to produce thirty-pounders (14 kg) each year. These are now being returned alive, so who knows what might turn up in the future.

In Staffordshire there are a couple of waters with big-pike potential. One is Stanley Pool, a heavily stocked fishery which has consistently produced pike of over 30 lb (14 kg) and several of 35 lb (16 kg). Not far from this water is the giant trout reservoir of Blithfield, which has also produced many thirty-pounders (14 kg). It looks set to throw up a much bigger fish, although many are now being removed. It is not easy to get permission to fish there and you are restricted to lure fishing.

In the Midlands there is Gailey Trout Fishery and Patshull Pool. Both are stocked with trout and on both waters the large pike are returned. If things continue to develop, my guess is that some big fish of over 30 lb (14 kg) will turn up.

In Norfolk the Thurne system needs no introduction, for it has the best record of any water for really big pike. However, some of the Bure Broads could grow a very big fish, so do not think that all the monster pike are in the Thurne. Lyng trout pit has also produced several fish of over 35 lb (16 kg), but angling pressure has increased so much on this water that the chances of any further giant pike must be reduced.

Further south still is Abberton Reservoir, a very big water with little in the way of fishable bank. It has produced many thirty pounders and could yet turn up a monster. The whole of Essex is dotted with productive gravel and chalk pits, several of which have consistently yielded 35 lb-plus (16 kg) fish. Tring reservoirs, in Hertfordshire, have also produced some big pike and though 32 lb

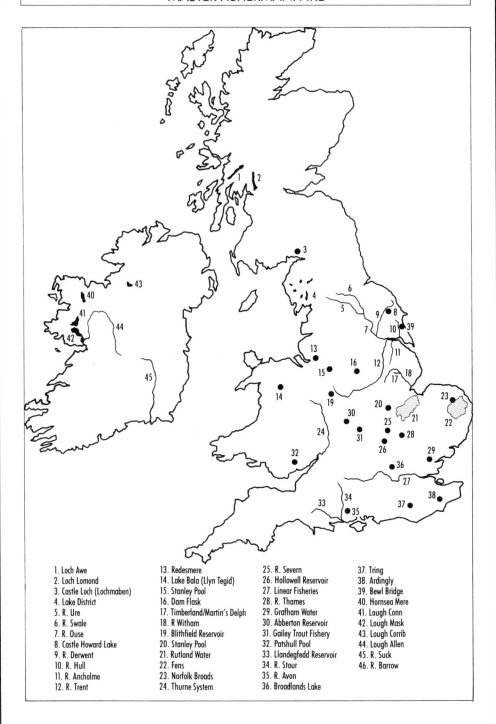

1. Loch Awe
2. Loch Lomond
3. Castle Loch (Lochmaben)
4. Lake District
5. R. Ure
6. R. Swale
7. R. Ouse
8. Castle Howard Lake
9. R. Derwent
10. R. Hull
11. R. Ancholme
12. R. Trent

13. Redesmere
14. Lake Bala (Llyn Tegid)
15. Stanley Pool
16. Dam Flask
17. Timberland/Martin's Delph
18. R Witham
19. Blithfield Reservoir
20. Stanley Pool
21. Rutland Water
22. Fens
23. Norfolk Broads
24. Thurne System

25. R. Severn
26. Hollowell Reservoir
27. Linear Fisheries
28. R. Thames
29. Grafham Water
30. Abberton Reservoir
31. Gailey Trout Fishery
32. Patshull Pool
33. Llandegfedd Reservoir
34. R. Stour
35. R. Avon
36. Broadlands Lake

37. Tring
38. Ardingly
39. Bewl Bridge
40. Hornsea Mere
41. Lough Conn
42. Lough Mask
43. Lough Corrib
44. Lough Allen
45. R. Suck
46. R. Barrow

(14.5 kg) seems to be the limit they cannot be discounted. There are several trout waters in Cambridgeshire, the best known of which is Grafham Water. This has sadly seen a great slaughter of pike, yet might yield the odd big one. Rutland Water, in Leicestershire, is bigger, but also suffers from pike removal.

Heading south-west to Hampshire, you have the Avon and the Stour. Both of these rivers turn up big pike and have produced fish of over 35 lb (16 kg). Broadlands Lake, in Hampshire, if a somewhat artificial water, is regularly stocked with big pike from trout waters and presents the angler with a chance of a really big fish.

Another southern trout water, Bewl Bridge, in Kent, has a big-pike reputation, but the use of gill-nets has seen the death of many fine fish. Ardingly, just north of Brighton, is a former trout water and this fishery continues to produce a few pike of over 30 lb (14 kg) every year. Whether it now has the potential to produce a thirty-five pounder (16 kg) is unclear.

Wales

Until Llandegfedd hit the headlines, Wales was not noted for big pike. This large trout reservoir yielded six fish of over 35 lb (16 kg), four of these over 40 lb (18 kg). The fact that the two latter were caught twice demonstrates the benefits of putting the fish back.

Ireland

Ireland still remains a good place to go on holiday, although there are some waters where visiting anglers have killed so many fish that it is not worth fishing. Waters such as Lough Corrib, Lough Allen, the River Barrow and River Suck have all in recent years produced very big pike. However, the problem facing the visitor is finding enough time to locate what is a very scarce commodity in any water.

Other reliable pike waters

Although the waters that impress us most are those that produce the biggest fish, not all anglers have the time, money or inclination to fish them. There are in any case many other venues that offer good pike fishing, despite the lack of huge fish. These waters, if fished seriously, should yield a twenty-pounder (9 kg).

Castle Loch, or Lochmaben as it is sometimes known, is a popular

Scottish venue for English anglers in the close season. The fishing is mainly from the bank. The water is also well known for its bream. It is not until you get down to Yorkshire that the pike fishing becomes comparable. The Ouse, Ure, Swale and Derwent have all yielded big pike in the past and although it takes a lot of effort, each of these waters will provide good sport with fish of over 10 lb (4.5 kg) and the chance of a twenty-pounder (9 kg). The River Hull, which runs from the Driffield area to Hull, is a chalk stream noted for its good pike fishing and much of it is free fishing, provided you have a Yorkshire Water Authority rod licence. Nearer the coast, but still near Hull, is Hornsea Mere, a 400-acre (160 hectares) water which is shallow but yields some big pike each year. Here it is mainly boat fishing, with some bank fishing.

To the west is Cheshire, with many large still-waters. Stoke Angling Club have stocked a lot of big pike into their waters such as Stanley Pool (see page 137) and Redesmere. This ought to give many anglers a good chance of a big pike. If you enjoy fishing in Wales, then try Llyn Tegid (Lake Bala). There are not many twenty-pounders (9 kg), but plenty of hard-fighting fish of over 10 lb (4.5 kg) make it worth visiting.

Lincolnshire has a lot of waters, although few are exceptional big-pike waters. You can, however, find some good rivers and drains that provide first-class winter fishing. The River Ancholme is controlled by Scunthorpe AC and regularly produces fish to 20 lb (9 kg). A little further south is the Witham, a long and interesting river with many feeder drains. When the river itself is in flood, pike frequently run up the drains to escape the dirty water.

Timberland, or Martin's Delph, is one well-known water which, although not as good as it was, may well provide the diligent angler with some good fish. Farther south, the River Welland has its own system of drains such as Vernatt's, which can absorb a lot of pike anglers without seeming crowded. Drains such as this have from time to time fished really well in the summer, which is not always the case in the Fens.

The Midlands has a host of reservoirs such as Hollowell, which is now run as a pike fishery by Andy Barker. Tickets to fish this water are available from Andy's shop in Coventry. Regular stocking with good fish ensures that there is always a chance of a big pike, along with the smaller native fish. We should not forget the Severn and the Trent, both excellent pike rivers. The weirpools are the place to start, and other areas, such as lock cuttings, are well worth a look.

Broadland

This area has been described in some detail earlier in the book, but the beginner should visit either the Bure at Wroxham or the Ormesby group of broads. Both can respond very well to deadbaits. I myself offer a guide service for visitors to the area and am more than happy to take people round these prolific waters.

Fenland proper, around Cambridge, has been in the doldrums in the past few years, but waters such as the River Delph still deserve a visit. Sadly, pike are much scarcer than they were, owing to competition from zander, but if you like to go after both, as I do, then you can still enjoy yourself. For easy access directly from the road, the Sixteen Foot still takes some beating. Most Fenland waters are now in the control of local clubs and you should first call into village shops or Post Offices for information.

Linear Fisheries in Bedfordshire is a wonderful place to start your pike fishing and for only £20 a year you have a huge expanse of water to try. They have recently stocked a thirty-seven-pounder (17 kg), so watch out! The Thames continues to offer good pike fishing, as do many of the southern rivers. For still-waters you would be well advised to contact Leisure Sport in Chertsey, Surrey, or ARC, who both control many southern waters, most of which have good-quality pike fishing.

One thing is certain and that is that the angler who fishes seriously and makes a big effort has got the chance of a fish of over 30 lb (14 kg). It may take many years, but it is not an impossible task. Even if you are devoted to catching a giant pike, do not forget to enjoy all the fish you catch. The initial run is the same, regardless of the size of the fish and it is that moment, when you wonder how big the pike is, that encapsulates my enjoyment of pike fishing.

INDEX

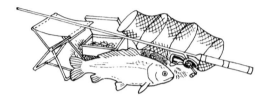

Page numbers in italics refer to illustrations

Photography Acknowledgments

All colour photographs provided by John Watson. All black and
white photographs provided by John Watson except for: page 21
Heather Angel/Biofotos; page 63 Ken Whitehead.